SONGS OF LATIN A[

From the Field to the Classroom

Canciones de América Latina: de sus orígenes a la escuela

by Patricia Shehan Campbell
with Ana Lucía Frega

*Your purchase benefits the International Society for Music Education (ISME),
which receives a portion of the sales.*

Editor: Gayle Giese
Text Editor: Nadine DeMarco
Spanish Text Editor: María A. Chenique
Editorial Assistant: Kristina Pusey
Classroom Recording Producer: Teena Chinn

Art Design and Layout: María A. Chenique
Music Engraver: Adrián Álvarez
Illustrations: Rama Hughes
Production Coordinator: Sharon Marlow

WARNER BROS. PUBLICATIONS
Warner Music Group
An AOL Time Warner Company
USA: 15800 NW 48th Avenue, Miami, FL 33014

WARNER/CHAPPELL MUSIC

CANADA: 15800 N.W. 48th AVENUE
MIAMI, FLORIDA 33014
SCANDINAVIA: P.O. BOX 533, VENDEVAGEN 85 B
S-182 15, DANDERYD, SWEDEN
AUSTRALIA: P.O. BOX 353
3 TALAVERA ROAD, NORTH RYDE N.S.W. 2113
ASIA: THE PENINSULA OFFICE TOWER, 12th FLOOR
18 MIDDLE ROAD
TSIM SHA TSUI, KOWLOON, HONG KONG

NUOVA CARISCH

ITALY: VIA CAMPANIA, 12
20098 S. GIULIANO MILANESE (MI)
ZONA INDUSTRIALE SESTO ULTERIANO
SPAIN: MAGALLANES, 25
28015 MADRID
FRANCE: CARISCH MUSICOM,
25, RUE D'HAUTEVILLE, 75010 PARIS

INTERNATIONAL MUSIC PUBLICATIONS LIMITED

ENGLAND: GRIFFIN HOUSE,
161 HAMMERSMITH ROAD, LONDON W6 8BS
GERMANY: MARSTALLSTR. 8, D-80539 MUNCHEN
DENMARK: DANMUSIK, VOGNMAGERGADE 7
DK 1120 KOBENHAVNK

Dedication

To singers, both young and old, that they might experience something of the spirit of Latin America through the musical nuances of these traditional songs.

Collaborators

Patricia Shehan Campbell is Donald E. Petersen professor of music at the University of Washington. She is author of this volume and numerous other books on music for children and teachers, including *Songs in Their Heads, Lessons From the World*, and *Music in Cultural Context*, and co-author of *Music in Childhood, Multicultural Perspectives in Music Education, Traditional Songs of Singing Cultures,* and collections of music from Vietnam, Cambodia, and China.

Ana Lucía Frega is doctora en pedagogía at the Universidad Nacional de San Martín, Argentina; member of the Academia Nacional de Educación of her country; and former president of the International Society for Music Education (1996–1998). She was the initiator of this project at the Amsterdam ISME meeting in 1996 and organizer and provider of continued energy and support to all involved in the project. Author of numerous books and articles on research in music education, Frega's best-known works include *Music for All, All for Music*; *Música para maestros*; and a collection of her own songs and poems.

Many thanks go to:

Chooi-Theng Lew, doctoral student of music education at the University of Washington, who provided transcriptions of words and music for "Adelita," "Chacarera," "El Rabel," and "Tamborcita."

María Lorena Filosa, Buenos Aires, Argentina, who translated the songs from Spanish to English so that further description and lessons could be devised.

Marcio Fonseca, who translated the Portuguese songs to English.

Gladys Cardona, for information on Guatemala.

María de León Arcila and Jorge Alberto Jara de León of La Escuela de Iniciación Musical Para Bebés y Niños Titita, Querétaro, Mexico, for "Adelita" and consultation along the way concerning this project.

Mireya Alegría of Santiago, Chile, for "El Rabel."

Ethel Batres (and musical associates) of Guatemala City, Guatemala, for "Tamborcito" and "El Barreño."

Teca A. Brito and Teca Oficina de Música of São Paulo, Brazil, for "Bambu" and "Cajueiro Pequenino."

Arturo Costas Guardia of La Paz, Bolivia, for "Viva Mi Patria Bolivia."

Michelle Amato, vocalist, for her renditions of "Arroz con Leche," "De Colores," and "Ma Teodora." These three recordings were produced at Gettings Productions Inc./Starke Lake Studios, Ocoee, Florida, with every possible attempt to match the authenticity of the other field recordings.

Teena Chinn, recording producer; Andy de Ganahl, recording engineer; Lindsey Blair, guitar; Teena Chinn, keyboards; Keith Wilson, percussion; and Michelle Amato, Michelle Lindhall, Elizabeth Ledger, and Rachael Farris, vocalists, for their work at Gettings Productions Inc./Starke Lake Studios, Ocoee, Florida, producing the classroom recordings.

Beatriz Sánchez of Paraná, Argentina, for "Chacarera."

Musicians of Camerata Folklórica Octavo En-Re-Do, Caracas, Venezuela, for "Llegó Diciembre."

Gary Louie, recording engineer for the University of Washington School of Music, for his work in mastering the field recordings.

Preface

This collection of twelve songs from the Caribbean and Central and South America is intended for use by teachers and their students in schools; by communities of singers who gather for every circumstance; for informal sings; for musical exposures and experiences; and for public performances. We hope to bridge a significant gap in the repertoire of songs for children, youth, and members of the adult singing community and to respond as teachers to the increased interest (but minimal information) worldwide in the musical expressions of Latin America. From a world perspective, such a collection of Latin American music and cultural considerations is long overdue.

The Declaration of Beliefs of the International Society for Music Education, developed by the Panel on World Musics (chaired by Bruno Nettl), stated in 1998 that "the musics of the world's cultures, seen individually and as a unit, should play a significant role in the field of music education, broadly defined." When acted upon, such a belief graduates from sentiment to valued use, and so we embarked upon this small collection of material over the course of several years. The field recordings occurred mostly in Mérida, Venezuela, when teachers gathered at an all-Latin America conference to sing songs of interest and meaning to them and citizens of their country. Some were children's songs, while others were traditional songs embraced by singers of every age. All were real songs, alive and well, rather than "artifact-songs" plucked from printed sources of days-gone-by. They are but a sample of the riches of these countries, and of the Latin American region at large, but they serve as entry-points to cultures that merit much more extensive exploration.

We suggest that listeners listen, listen-and-sing, sing-and-dance, dance-and-then-read about the songs and the people who sing them. For those who know little Spanish, these songs will bring the nuances of the language to their ears. For those who wish to know a bit more of the world, these songs are gateways to cultural studies. For those who love music, these songs give more music to love.

Patricia Shehan Campbell
Seattle, Washington, U.S.A.

Ana Lucía Frega
Buenos Aires, Argentina

Special Features and Instructional Uses for This Book and CD

This project promises to give insights and experiences that will benefit teachers, students (from the very young to the continuing adult student), listeners, and singers. It is a one-of-a-kind project that offers field recordings of singers from nine nations in Latin America, including South and Central America and the Caribbean. Look for 🌐 to identify CD tracks for the field recordings. Also included are childrens' classroom recordings 📓 . Descriptive notes discuss the nine nations and twelve songs, and make suggestions for their use in the classroom and community.

But as far as Latin American music goes, is this project really unique? On one hand, there have been numerous scholarly works on musical cultures of Latin America. Beyond the highly technical dissertations, there are many works for the interested reader: Robert Stevenson's 1952 classic work, *Music in Mexico: A Historical Survey*; John Storm Roberts' well-used survey of *The Latin Tinge: The Impact of Latin American Music on the United States* (1978); *The Brazilian Sound: Samba, Bossa Nova and the Popular Music of Brazil* by Chris McGowan and Ricardo Pessanha (1991); Tom Turino's 1993 study of the music of the Peruvian Altiplano, *Moving Away From Silence*; Ercilia Moreno Chá's 1995 work, *Tango Tuyo, Mío, y Nuestro*; and the compendium of essays edited by John M. Schecter on regional traditions in *Music in Latin American Culture* (1999). Some of these works are accompanied by recordings, although there are few songs appropriate for singing, and they are neither recorded nor transcribed.

On the other hand, collections of Latin American songs meant to be sung have been published in English-speaking countries such as the United States, but none take singers—or their teachers—into Latin American musical cultures as far as they might. There are songs without accompanying recordings, songs with piano accompaniments in lieu of guitar or other indigenous instruments, songs with "singing translations" in English or other languages, songs with singing voices trained far beyond the quality of the common singer, and songs that feature adult rather than children's voices. This book and CD address some of these shortcomings by offering songs easily singable by children and using indigenous instruments in the recordings.

This project is unique, then, in numerous ways: in its aim at gathering singers from different Latin American nations to perform one or two representative traditional songs from their culture, in making available the recordings of these singers, in preparing readable and singable transcriptions of the songs, and in providing arrangements for instruments typically found in school classrooms and in some community settings. In addition to the songs, the cultures to which the songs belong are described, and suggestions for their instructional use by teachers and community musicians are included. The cultural descriptions lay out contextual information regarding the songs. Knowledge of typical traditional dress, roles of family members, recreational interests, food preferences, and holiday celebrations may help develop a deeper understanding of factors that motivate the musical form, function, instruments, and song verse. Such knowledge could be fuel for setting the song into a larger unit of study: beyond the song to the songmakers themselves. The cultural information is provided in general terms; by no means do we intend to stereotype a particular group or culture.

The teaching suggestions are meant to spark ideas for the use of these songs by teachers: music specialists, classroom teachers, language arts and social studies teachers. Add to this musicians who work in the community, including settings that draw children and youth in after-school programs, weekend events, camp settings, and church-affiliated groups as well as adult singers who simply wish to extend their repertoire in informal "sings." The teaching suggestions include activities that spring from Dalcroze-oriented movement (given that the author is a certified Dalcroze teacher), Kodaly-inspired singing exercises (corresponding to the author's work as guest instructor in Kodaly training programs), and Orff-styled instrumental classroom arrangements. These instrumental arrangements follow the teaching suggestions for each song, except on "Llegó Diciembre," in which the arrangement precedes the suggestions. The songs can be sung alone, with the recording, with guitar-only accompaniment, and with rhythmic unpitched and pitched classroom percussion instruments. The songs can be used with a geography lesson or a discussion of cultural values and practices, and they also can lead to further exploration of musical and cultural expressions.

This volume is based on the idea that musical traditions outside our own require careful listening. Thus, the recording (CD) is key to the performance of these pieces. Adults and children alike are the performers, and since the sounds of the language and music are in their ears, they know best the nuances to preserve and transmit. The field recordings are as authentic as possible and do not always project a perfectly musical performance, but should be valued for their authenticity. The classroom recordings were created in a studio situation and provide a good model for children's in-tune singing; the instrumental accompaniment was performed by professional musicians who used the classroom instrumental arrangements shown in this book and improvised upon them. Students may play along with these recordings. All the recordings deserve repeated listenings by those who would wish to sing these songs—not just three or four times, but many times, until the sounds begin to permeate, to sink beneath the surface of the skin, to reach the listener's inner ear and the mind that processes the music. These songs deserve to be danced and moved to, to have their musical segments dissected into parts as large as a refrain or as small as an interval; their words and linguistic idioms should be examined for the techniques needed to be able to sing and play these pieces. But performances begin and end with listening, so the CD can be used alone or with the book, but the book cannot stand alone without the recording. Listening is the launch to performance, and a return to listening once the song is learned is a built-in means of assessing the success of performers in matching the model.

Classroom Instruments Suggested With Lesson Plans in This Book

 Bass Drum

 Bell Tree

 Bongos

 Claves

 Conga

 Cowbell

 Guiro

 Guitar

 Hand Drum

 Maracas (Llama's Hooves)

 Ratchet

 Snare Drum

 Tambourine

 Wood Block

SG – Soprano Glockenspiel
AG – Alto Glockenspiel
SX – Soprano Xylophone
AX – Alto Xylophone
BX – Bass Xylophone
SM – Soprano Metallophone
AM – Alto Metallophone
BM – Bass Metallophone

Contents

About Latin American Cultures

Latin America is a massive geographic region encompassing the South American continent, Central America, Mexico (which is a part of North America), and the islands of the Caribbean Sea. The varied geographic features and climates of Latin America encompass the diverse histories of its peoples and their unique cultures and circumstances. Still, the designation of Latin or Latin American is given to a broad sweep of the world's population, as if these groups are all the same.

Latin Americans typically feel pride in their local or national collective culture and hold allegiances to their nation that often override a sense of an overall Latin identity. A Chilean is first and foremost a citizen of Chile, a product of values and lifestyle local to Santiago (or whatever Chilean city or town he claims as home), and only afterward is he categorized, and usually by outsiders, as "Latin."

Yet despite the many cultures, countries, and geographic regions, there are a number of striking features that unite Latin America. Many Latin American countries were settled by the Spanish beginning in the sixteenth century; Brazil's colonization by Portugal is among the few prominent exceptions. Following three centuries of Spanish or Portuguese rule, many countries sought and achieved independence and established themselves as free states. The influence of the Iberian people remain, however, in language and religion and in certain customs and courtesies that were brought long ago from the old country and adapted and shaped to the needs of the new country. The practice of embracing when greeting family and friends is widely prevalent throughout Latin American countries, as is the use of gestures to punctuate conversation, the close physical proximity of people during conversation, and the tendency to touch (arms, sleeve, hand, back) to maximize communication. The celebration of certain religious holidays (for example, Christmas and Semana Santa [Holy Week]) is commonplace, as is the tendency for cities and towns to honor their patron saint with festivals and religious services.

The presence of people of various ethnicities is a common feature as well. In addition to the Spanish, Portuguese, and other European influences, there are also contributions by indigenous (Native or First) peoples as well as Africans who were brought to the region mostly as slaves for plantations in the eighteenth and nineteenth centuries. These groups shaped the character of individual nations. The cultural expressions of Bolivia, for example, are strongly influenced by the Native majority, while Cuba's notable African population has shaped cultural expressions in that country. A new group also arose as different ethnicities intermarried to create a unique mestizo, or blended, population.

A country's economy depends on many variables, not the least of which is geographic location and climate, as well as a stable government. Cuisine varies, too, also for reasons of climate, although rice, beans, and salsa are prominent in many parts of Latin America. Families tend to be solid, supportive, and stable, and men are usually the head of the household. For recreation, playing or watching soccer is nearly a constant across the nations, while visiting family and friends, watching television, and participating in festivals of music and dance seem also to be popular activities of Latin Americans. Yet all of Latin American culture cannot be defined as a single entity. It is diverse, many-splendored, and rich in cultures and cultural expressions.

About Latin American Musics

The many musical expressions found in South and Central America and in the Caribbean merit making the word "music" plural, to "musics." This volume would therefore appropriately cover the subject of Latin American musics. For how could African-inspired styles of Puerto Rico and Cuba be thought of in the same way as a Bolivian melody for guitars and flutes? How could a Guatemalan marimba piece be compared to an Argentine chacarera melody? Merengue and mariachi are distant forms from one another, and the music of Brazilian samba schools are in no way related to Chile's nueva canción. The diversity of Latin American musics is its many forms and its wide variety of instruments, topical texts, languages, poetic structures, and relevant dance forms. Because music is a reflection of cultural surroundings, behaviors, and values, there will be distinctive musical traditions. The descendents of the Native Americans, Europeans, and Africans who live in Latin America have maintained aspects of their musical roots and contributed to new musical blends.

Themes can be traced through the different musical expressions of Latin America. Found throughout the large region are songs of love, deeply felt, passionately expressed, and tinged with longing, loneliness, and unrequited love. There are the songs that tell stories or convey historic and current events, from the Mexican corrido to the Chilean "nueva canción." Songs link the singer to the supernatural, from the female shaman singers among the Mapuche of Chile to the drumming, dancing, and chanting of the candomblé—believers of Afro-Brazilian bahia. These themes are not so thoroughly integrated within the musical traditions of other cultures of the world but are evident in the musical repertoire of Latin Americans. Add to these themes the more universally accepted genres such as children's songs, songs of the seasons, and descriptive songs in tribute to specific individuals, and Latin American cultures begin to show their connectedness through their music.

Similar instruments, melodies, and rhythms also unite Latin American musics. The guitar is prominent in the music of most Latin cultures, particularly those rooted in Hispanic traditions. Maracas are commonplace in the Caribbean, Venezuela, Mexico, and Brazil, and the clave and guiro are largely Caribbean but find their way under different names and slightly different constructions into the Brazilian samba and the Argentine tango. Drums are important to Latin Americans, including the single-headed drum of the Aymara and Quechua of the Andes region and the ensemble of drums found in Brazil and Cuba. Minor-keyed melodies are frequently found, as are rhythms that cross between a feeling of threes and twos. Pentatonic melodies are more the norm than not (especially in the musics of Native Americans and many mestizo peoples), and syncopations abound in the music of African-inspired genres from Cuba to Brazil. Also, Latin American musics incite bodies to dance, whether communally in the round or with partners moving their bodies in precise synchrony.

But why not listen and experience first-hand the variety of Latin American musics and the subtle bonds among them? To do so will underscore the diverse yet interrelated forms and nuances of musical expression in Latin America.

Argentina

"Don't Cry for Me, Argentina," a song intended to personify the character of Eva Perón, the wife of former Argentine president, Juan Domingo Perón, is what may come to the minds of non-Argentines when they think of music and Argentina. Or maybe the tango, the popular dance of the Río de la Plata region (including Buenos Aires), with its intricate patterns of suave and sophisticated men and women on a ballroom floor. But Argentine music, like the history and cultural composite of Argentina itself, is much more than this. It is a myriad of folk and traditional genres, an art music world of its own, and a colorful scene for popular music forms that stretch far beyond the image offered by *Evita*'s soundtrack.

The Musical Surroundings: Getting to Know Argentina

Land and People. Argentina is a land with many rivers. Its name derives from *argent,* meaning "silver." This term refers to its rivers that shine silver in the sun as they flow to the sea from the towering Andes mountains that form Argentina's western border with Chile. Before the Spanish began to colonize Argentina in the 1500s, the area was populated by various indigenous groups, including Incans, as well as nomadic and autonomous groups. Spain ruled the region until a revolution erupted in 1810, and independence was finally declared for Argentina in 1816. Today's Argentine population includes mestizos (Spanish and aboriginal mix), Italians, Germans, Japanese, Jews, French, and Russians, comprising a broad multicultural population in the capital city, Buenos Aires, and well beyond it. The Argentine Republic has 23 provinces and one federal district (Buenos Aires) and a culture as rich as its geography—from coastal plains to las pampas (the central plains) to waterfalls, glaciers, and mountains.

Economy. Agriculture, which employs about 10 percent of the people, and industry are vital parts of the economy. Argentina is a major exporter of beef, hides, and wool, as well as large amounts of wheat, corn, and flaxseed. Its industries include food processing, meatpacking, motor vehicles, textiles, and metallurgy.

Education. School is compulsory and free from ages six through fourteen. Secondary and higher education are also free but require an entrance examination; nearly three-fourths of all eligible students are enrolled in secondary school. Argentina's adult literacy rate of 97 percent is one of the highest in Latin America.

Language. Spanish is the official language of Argentina, although accents vary by region. The most distinctive is the porteño (Buenos Aires) accent, which has been influenced by Italian. "Y" and "ll" are pronounced as "sh" in porteño, so that *llamar* ("to call") sounds more like "shah-mahr" than the typical "yah-mahr."

Customs and Courtesies. Argentines greet each other by shaking hands and nodding slightly to show respect. In urban areas, a brief embrace with a kiss on the cheek is also common. "Buenos días" (good morning) ("buen día" in Buenos Aires) or "buenas tardes" (good afternoon) are common greetings, and for formal situations, titles are customary—"señor" or "don" and "señora" or "doña"—for men and women, respectively. Argentines tend to use hand gestures to supplement verbal communication and may use gestures to communicate at a distance. (For example, to order a cup of coffee in a restaurant from a distance, it is appropriate to hold up an extended thumb and index finger separated slightly, with the other fingers folded into a fist.) Individuals stand closer together than in other cultures during conversation, and eye contact and some touching of the arms is standard. Yawning without covering the mouth is impolite, as is placing one's hands on one's hips.

Appearance. In Buenos Aires, European and North American fashions are popular (with preference given to North American styles). Older women seldom wear pants, but the younger generation prefers dressing more casually. Outside the city, the dress reflects regional culture; for example, the gauchos (cowboys) of las pampas wear wide-brimmed hats, neckerchiefs, bombachas (wide-legged pants), and boots.

Families. Urban families tend to be rather small, averaging two children, but rural families are larger. The responsibility of raising children and managing household finances falls on the mother. Women working outside the home comprise less than 30 percent of the workforce, but men often work well into the evening (often returning home after 9 p.m.). Families will sacrifice much to give their children a good education.

Recreation. Soccer (fútbol) is the national sport enjoyed by adults and children, and a typical weekend will feature a game of soccer. Other popular sports include basketball, volleyball, and rugby. Buenos Aires is home to a fine opera house (the Colón), movies, restaurants, and clubs. The tango is enjoying a revival among some young adults, and many enjoy dancing and listening to music from the United States, Brazil, and Central America. Older men often play chess or bochas (lawn bowling) in public squares.

Food. Beef is preferred by Argentines, even at lunchtime. Asados, or barbecues, are common weekend activities. Other foods include empanadas (meat or vegetable turnovers) and locro (a winter stew of meat, corn, and potatoes).

Holidays. Christmas Eve is widely celebrated by Argentines. The extended family gathers at 9 p.m. for dinner, music, dancing, and opening gifts from Papá Noel (Father Christmas). Pastries and candies are served before midnight, and then fireworks begin. New Year's Day is another festival of fireworks. Other holidays include the Anniversary of the May Revolution (May 25); Independence Day (July 9); Death of General José de San Martín, who is known as the Liberator of Peru, Chile, and Argentina for his defeat of the Spanish in 1812 (August 17); and Student Day (September 21), the first day of spring, which is marked by picnics, visits to the park, and soccer games.

Chacarera
(Dance, for the Girl of the Hills)

About the Song

For every group of people, there are multiple genres of songs. Functions vary, too, including those that express love, celebrate holidays, accompany religious rituals and ceremonies, mourn the dead, gather people in solidarity, and bring imaginary characters to life. Those who sing "Chacarera" in Argentina, however, intend it as a silly song. It tells of a young farm girl in the hills who is told to take care of her farm so that the doves don't mess it up, and whose hens lay eggs (as if that is great news!). It is rhythmically playful, a musical match for the nonsensical text.

The chacarera is a folk dance of Argentina dating from the mid-nineteenth century and still danced in northern Argentina. It is a loosely formed couples dance that features toe-tapping (zapateado), syncopated rhythm, and often the sound of one or two bomba drums. The chacarera includes a rhythmic feature called sesquiáltera (changing sixes), a 6/8 metrical feel that alternates with a 3/4 emphasis. Beatriz Sánchez sings the song on the recording ⑬ and accompanies herself on the guitar.

Chacarera

Argentina

Wait for guitar intro.

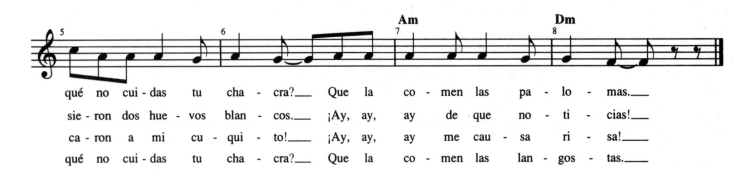

Verse 1:

Chacarera, chacarera,
Chah-kah-reh-rah, chah-kah-reh-rah
Chacarera de las lomas,
Chah-kah-reh-rah day lahs loh-mahs
¿Por qué no cuidas tu chacra?
Por kay no kwee-dahs too chak-rah
Que la comen las palomas.
Kay lah koh-men lahs pah-loh-mahs.

Verse 2:

Una gallinita blanca
Oo-nah gah-yee-nee-tah blahn-kah
Y otra de color ceniza,
Yoh-trah day koh-lohr sehr-nee-sah
Pusieron dos huevos blancos.
Poo-syehr-own dohs hway-vohs blahn-kohs
Ay, ay, ay de que noticias!
I yi yi day kay noh-tee-see-yahs.

Verse 3:

Una gallinita blanca
Oo-nah gah-yee-nee-tah blahn-kah
Y otra de color ceniza,
Yoh-trah day koh-lohr sehr-nee-sah
Picaron a mi cuquito!
Pee-kah-rohn ah mee koo-kee-toh
Ay, ay, ay me causa risa!
I yi yi may kaw-sah ree-sah

Verse 4:

Chacarera, chacarera,
Chah-kah-reh-rah, chah-kah-reh-rah
Chacarera de las boscas,
Chah-kah-reh-rah day lahs bohs-kahs
¿Por qué no cuidas tu chacra?
Por kay no kwee-dahs too chak-rah
Que la comen las langostas.
Kay lah koh-men lahs lahn-goh-stahs.

Text in English

Verse 1:

Chacarera, Chacarera, young girl of the hills,
Why don't you take care of your farm
So the doves don't mess it up.

Verse 2:

A little white hen and another ash-colored one
Laid two white eggs.
Oh, what news to tell!

Verse 3:

A little white hen and another ash-colored one
Bit my dog!
Oh, it makes me laugh!

Verse 4:

Chacarera, Chacarera, young girl of the forest,
Why don't you take care of your farm
So that it's eaten by the locusts.

Teaching Suggestions

1. Trace the mountainous region of the southern cone of South America on a map, noting the location of the Andes along the western edge and northern region of Argentina. Ask students to find the capital, Buenos Aires, at the mouth of the Río de la Plata. Follow the line of mountains from the southern tip at Tierra del Fuego up past Mendoza and Córdoba to Tucumán. Imagine with students a farm in the hills where cows are kept and chickens and sheep are raised: this is the setting for the chacarera (the dance) and the song "Chacarera."

2. Describe aspects of Argentine life, and consider the difference between living in Buenos Aires and in a northern Argentine town with regard to family income, schooling, and recreation.

Relate to students' understanding of the difference between rural and urban lifestyles in their own experience.

3. Listen to the recording of "Chacarera" and try to hear the quick six pulses per measure and the divisions of them into three groups of two pulses each and two groups of three pulses each.

4. Listen to Spanish words that sound more than once: "chacarera" (dance), "gallinita blanca" (little white hen), "color ceniza" (ash-colored), "¿por qué?" (why?), "ay-ay-ay" (oh my). Display the words on the board or overhead projector, and practice pronouncing them.

5. Learn to sing the song through consistent listening and repeated attempts to sing it, stopping on occasion to listen to and imitate selected phrases.

6. Practice singing the melody on a neutral syllable such as "loo" to get a sense of the musical flow. Sing the melody on solfège, beginning with "re" for "D," and notice the stepwise scale movement of pitches at the beginning of the song.

7. While singing the melody without and then with text, pat the rhythm of the clave part. When students are comfortable with that part, experiment with singing and patting the maracas' and drum's parts. This will take time to coalesce singing voices with the rhythmic patterns, and it may be necessary to divide the group into several small groups: singers and three rhythm groups.

8. Once students can sing the song in a rhythmically accurate manner, try a zapateado accompaniment by stepping with the toe, heel, or whole foot on the accents in twos and threes.

9. As students get into the swing of the song, they will be ready to take on the accompaniment for xylophones and metallophones. Students may do well to work off the pattern of the claves that they have learned, recognizing that it matches the rhythm of the xylophones. Gradually put pitched and unpitched instruments together with the singing voices.

10. Learn to sing all four verses. Consider using the introduction as an instrumental interlude between verses, or play the entire verse on only instruments in between each sung verse.

11. The song can be suitably performed with guitars and bomba drums. In the case of the guitar strum, follow the rhythm of the maracas, playing a strong downstroke for each accented note and a more soft (and partial) stroke for the unaccented notes.

12. Students deserve to know more about Argentina and its musical and cultural expressions. Explore recordings for examples of chacarera, milonga, tonada, and the tango dance. Encourage students to locate Argentines with whom they might have conversations and interviews about music in contemporary life.

Chacarera

Classroom Instrumental Arrangement

Argentina

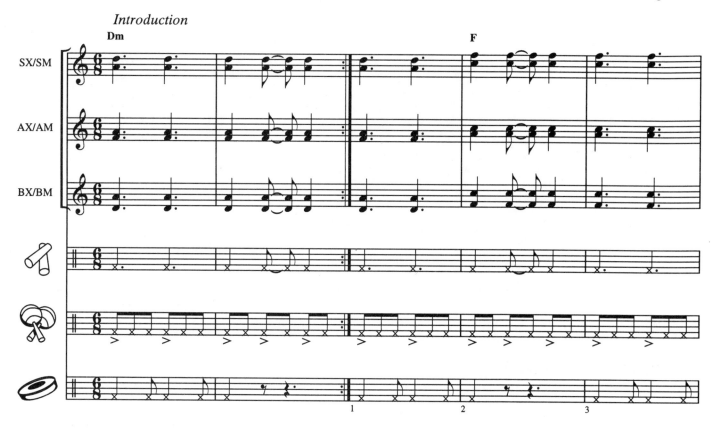

Bolivia

Bolivia evokes images of pipes, panpipes, charangos, guitars, and bomba drums played by cape-clad indígenas with black felt bowler hats. Whether the setting is a village high in the snow-capped Andes mountains, a downtown plaza in a North American city, or the entrance to a train station somewhere in Europe, the sound of Andean musicians from Bolivia (or Peru or Ecuador) playing pentatonic music in duple meter is appealing to listeners the world over. They play waynos that date from the sixteenth century on their zampoñas (panpipes, also called antara or siku) and quena (simple notched-end flutes). It is music that stirs the soul, expressions of romantic verse set to melodies that sadden, stimulate, or send the singer soaring as high as a condor. Bolivia's music mirrors its surroundings, including the land, the history, and the current conditions of its people.

The Musical Surroundings: Getting to Know Bolivia

Land and People. Located in the heart of South America, Bolivia is a land-locked country about three times the size of Montana with three distinct geographical areas: the high, cold altiplano (high plateau); the valles (valleys); and the llanos (wet forestlands) in the east. The indigenous Aymara were conquered by the Incan armies in the 1400s, and by 1538 the Spanish had achieved full control of the region. Political uprisings were frequent in the 1700s, but it was not until 1825 that the area gained independence from Spain and was named after its liberator, Simón Bolívar. Nearly 70 percent of Bolivians are Native Americans, including Quechua (30 percent) and Aymara (25 percent); another 25 percent are criollo of mixed indigenous Aymara and Quechua and European heritage, and another 5 percent are European. Bolivia is led by a president and El Congreso Nacional, whose aim is to reduce poverty, eliminate drug trafficking, and end corruption. The famous Lake Titicaca, the highest navigable body of water in the world (12,500 feet) and the mineral-rich Andes continue their formidable impression on the lives of Bolivians, shaping who they are, what they do, and how they are developing as large and small cultures within a modern nation.

Economy. Bolivia is one of the poorest and least developed Latin American countries. Half of the labor force is engaged in agriculture, including the harvest of coca and coffee. Mining, however, is its major industry, with natural resources such as tin, natural gas, gold, silver, and crude oil found with greatest frequency.

Education. School is free and compulsory for ages six to fourteen. The adult literacy rate is 84 percent (it is highest among men in urban areas). Less than half of all children complete their primary education, and only about one-third go on to secondary school. Educational reforms now permit bilingual education in Spanish and Native dialects where once only Spanish was permitted.

Language. Castellano (Spanish), Quechua (the language of the Incans), and Aymara are the official languages of Bolivia. Spanish is used in government and business.

Customs and Courtesies. Spanish-speaking Bolivians greet friends and acquaintances with a cheerful "buenos días." "Hola" (hi) or "¿Cómo estás?" ("How are you?") are also common. The titles "señor" (Mr.), "señora" (Mrs.), or "señorita" ("Miss") are added for first-time introductions or when greeting strangers, and "don or "doña" are added for respect before the first names of people ("Don Alfredo," "Doña María"). Bolivians stand close during conversation. Close friends and relatives greet with an abrazo, a combination of a hug, a handshake, two or three pats on the shoulder, and another handshake. Female friends often embrace and kiss each other on the cheek. Eye contact in conversation is essential, and to avoid it shows suspicion or lack of trust. To beckon children, one waves the fingers with the palm down, and a "no" is indicated with a waving of the index finger.

Appearance. Bolivians wear different clothing depending on where they live and their social class. Urban residents wear Western-style clothing. Many women wear a pollera (a full, colorful skirt), and rural women add a shawl called a manta. Both men and women may wear their hair braided under their bowler derby hats. Indigenous men might wear shin-length pants, a shirt, a thick leather belt, a poncho, and a hat. Women carry babies on their backs in an aguayo, a woven square cloth.

Families. The family is central to Bolivian people. It is typical to have one or two children in middle- and upperclass families, while poorer families are traditionally larger (although children often die in infancy). Most women work in the home, and it is difficult and time-consuming work without modern conveniences. While the father makes most family decisions, the mother exerts much influence on household affairs. The elderly live with their children's families.

Recreation. Soccer (fútbol) is popular throughout Bolivia. Leisure activities include watching television (in urban areas), visiting with friends, and attending festivals. Dancing and singing are popular at various events, and in the Chaco region, people get together to drink several rounds of hierba mate, an herbal tea.

Food. Potatoes, rice, soup, milk products, and fruit are commonly consumed by Bolivians. Potatoes are staples in the Altiplano, as is corn in the valleys and yucca in the lowlands. Most foods are fried and seasoned with llajua (a spicy salsa). Chicken is the most common meat.

Holidays. The year's celebrations are New Year's Day; Carnaval (Saturday before Ash Wednesday); Día del Mar, or Sea Day (March 23); Holy Week before Easter; Father's Day (March 19); Mother's Day (May 27); Independence Day (August 6); All Saints' Day (November 1, a day for the family to clean and decorate ancestral graves and enjoy a picnic); and Christmas. Children put their old shoes in a window for Papá Noel (Santa Claus) to take them in exchange for new gifts. Children also receive gifts on January 6 (Three Kings' Day). Dancing, wearing costumes, and pouring water on people are common during Carnaval, and a favorite treat at this festival is candy stuffed with nuts or fruit, called confite.

Viva Mi Patria Bolivia
Long Live My Homeland, Bolivia

About the Song

Every nation has songs that pay tribute to it and that allow people to express their allegiance, dedication, and love of their homeland. For Bolivians, "Viva Mi Patria Bolivia" is an expression of their commitment to their land. The sentiment extends beyond the countryside to a total commitment by Bolivians to the spirit of the land, including the long-standing and changing ways of Bolivians.

Arturo Costas Guardia of La Paz, Bolivia, sings and accompanies himself on the guitar in the recorded selection ⊉. The guitar (guitarra, guitarrón, guitarilla) is the most common instrument in Hispanic America, and in its acoustic form, it is played with an intensity seldom found in other parts of the world. The strumming is often organized in intricate ways, with full strums followed by partial strums, a passage of bass or treble pitches occasionally sounding (for example, during the interludes), and—just when the listener becomes accustomed to the musical flow—a change in texture or meter, or even the direction of the strum, may occur. Bolivians play guitars alone, in ensemble, and with violins, flutes, panpipes, and bomba drums.

Viva Mi Patria Bolivia

Bolivia

Wait for guitar intro.

1. Vi - va mi pa - tria, Bo - li - via,
2. Es - ta can - ción que yo can - to La
3. La lle - vo_____ en mi co - ra - zón, Y_le
4. Lai…

u - na gran na - ción.
brin - do con a - mor.
doy mi_ins - pi - ra - ción.

Por e - lla, doy_____ mi vi - da,
A mi pa - tria_____ Bo - li - via,
Quie_ra a mi pa - tria Bo - li - via,

Tam - bién mi co - ra - zón.
Que quie - ro con pa - sión.
Co - mo la quie - ro yo.

Por e - lla, doy_____ mi vi - da,
A mi pa - tria_____ Bo - li - via,
Quie_ra a mi pa - tria Bo - li - via,

Tam - bién mi co - ra - zón.
Que quie - ro con pa - sión.
Co - mo la quie - ro yo.

The Song Text

Verse 1:

Viva mi patria, Bolivia,
Vee-vah mee pah-tree-ah Boh-lee-vee-ah

Una gran nación.
Oo-nah grahn nah-syohn.

Por ella, doy mi vida,
Por ay-yah doy ee mee vee-dah

Tambien mi corazón. *(repeat lines 3–4)*
Tahm-bee-ehn mee koh-rah-sohn.

Verse 2:

Esta canción que yo canto
Ehs-tah kahn-cee-yon kay yoh kahn-toh

La brindo con amor.
Lah breen-doh kohn ah-mohr.

A mi patria, Bolivia,
Ah mee pah-tree-ah Boh-lee-vee-ah

Que quiero con pasión. *(repeat lines 3–4)*
Kay kee-eh-roh kohn pah-see-yohn.

Verse 3:

La llevo en mi corazón
Lah yay-voh ehn mee koh-rah-sohn

Y le doy mi inspiración.
Ee leh doy mee een-spee-rah-see-yohn.

Quiera a mi patria, Bolivia
Kee-eh-rah a mee pah-tree-ah Boh-lee-vee-ah

Como la quiero yo.
Koh-moh lah kee-yeh-roh yoh.

Verse 4:

Lai . . . *(for first two lines)*
Lahy

Quiera a mi patria, Bolivia
Kee-eh-rah ah mee pah-tree-ah Boh-lee-vee-ah

Como la quiero yo.
Koh-moh lah kee-yeh-roh yoh.

Text in English

Verse 1:

Long live my homeland, Bolivia,
A great nation.
For her, I would give my life,
And also my heart.

Verse 2:

This song that I sing
I offer with love
To my homeland, Bolivia,
That I love with passion.

Verse 3:

I have her in my heart,
And I give her my inspiration.
(I hope all will) love my homeland, Bolivia,
As I love her.

Verse 4:

Lai . . . *(for first two lines)*
(I hope all will) love my homeland, Bolivia,
As I love her.

Teaching Suggestions

1. Find Bolivia, a country in the west-central part of South America, on a map. Ask students to respond to questions about its location (surrounded by Peru, Brazil, Paraguay, Argentina, and Chile), its natural resources, and its economy.

2. Independently or as a group project, find photos in books and on the Web of Bolivia and Bolivians. Make a collage of them on poster board, dedicate a bulletin board to them, or develop a succession of overheads, slides, or video-splices that stimulate the singing of a nationalistic song like "Viva Mi Patria Bolivia."

3. Listen to the recording of "Viva Mi Patria Bolivia" and sway to the two feel of the 6/8 meter. Or try pat-clap-clap, pat-clap-clap (lightly) to the six beats per measure. Or conduct the meter in two and in six. Discuss the difference between conducting two beats per measure and conducting six beats per measure.

4. Listen for words that can be added to students' knowledge of Spanish, and that may help the learning of the song text: "Viva" (long live), "patria" (homeland, country), "nación" (nation), "vida" (life), "corazón" (heart), "canción" (song), "amor" (love), "pasión" (passion, emotion, sentiment). Practice pronouncing these words.

5. Sing the song's melody on "loo" before adding words. When singing the song text, start by singing just the words that students have learned to pronounce and singing "loo" on the others. Add other words, gradually working through the four verses.

6. Play the chords on guitar (with a basic strum that sounds twice per measure) while singing the song. Try playing the melody on recorders along with the guitar chording, and add the rhythmic ostinato on drum with soft, padded mallet and llamas' hooves (maracas can be substituted).

7. Learn the xylophone accompaniment, and layer in bass, then alto, then soprano xylophones.

8. Perform with singers and xylophonists, or singers and guitarists, or alternate these two accompaniments over the four verses. As interludes, consider performing the melody on recorder. Include drum and hooves (or maracas) throughout.

9. Listen to music from the high Andes, including combinations of guitars with violins, flute (quena), and panpipes (siku, zampoñas, anatara). Contact Andean musicians in the community, and arrange for students to attend a live performance.

Viva Mi Patria Bolivia

Classroom Instrumental Arrangement

Bolivia

All measures ostinati
(play same pattern throughout)

(llama's hooves)

Brazil

What is Brazil if not the country of Carnaval and the samba? Brazil is costumed dancers sparkling with glitter and topped with feathered and beaded headdresses. Brazil is the Bahian blocos afros (a black Carnaval group in Bahia) of drummers, and players of wood and beaded percussion instruments, stepping in time down the street to the cross-rhythms they play. It is also the Amazonian jungle, complete with exotic tropical plants and wildlife, and the beaches of Rio de Janeiro and Recife, lined with palm trees and tanned bodies. It is the citizens of the ultra-modern capital city of Brasília, the candomblé-believers of Bahia, the fashionably dressed residents of São Paulo, the landless living in favelas (shantytowns) outside Salvador, and the immigrants from Japan, Germany, Italy, and Lebanon spread across the country. It is people proud of their Brazilian way, warm, fun-loving, and free-spirited, where music and dance, as much as religion and food, define their national and regional identities.

The Musical Surroundings: Getting to Know Brazil

Land and People. Larger than the continental United States and comprising half of South America, Brazil is the fifth largest country in the world. Forests cover two-thirds of Brazil's territory, including the largest tropical rain forest in the Amazon River Basin. Brazil was inhabited by various groups when the Portuguese arrived in 1500, followed by the French and Dutch who also attempted to establish colonies there. Spain conquered Portugal from 1580 to 1640, but colonization by Portugal was in full swing after 1650. Dom Pedro I of Portugal declared Brazil's independence in 1822, although it was not until his son, Dom Pedro II, was deposed by an 1889 military coup that the country became independent. The military has seized control of the country five times since then, but today Brazil is a federative republic, consisting of 26 states and the federal district of Brasília. About 55 percent of Brazilians are of European (mostly Portuguese) descent, while 38 percent are mixed heritage and 6 percent are black African descent, with about 200,000 indigenous people living in the Amazon region. The country lies south of the equator and has a mostly tropical climate, except in the southernmost area where freezing temperatures are possible. From the lush rain forest of the north to the grasslands and savannas of the west to the farms and factories of the south, Brazil boasts tremendous diversity in its topography, economy, and ethnicity.

Economy. Brazil has the largest economy in South America and the ninth largest in the world. Still, income distribution is unequal, and poverty affects more than one-third of the population. Brazil is self-sufficient in food and consumer goods and is the world's largest producer of coffee, oranges, and bananas. It also is a major producer of soybeans, corn, and cocoa. The industrial sector exports automobiles and parts, textiles, steel, and metals. Natural resources include gold, nickel, tin, oil, and timber.

Education. Children complete eight years of compulsory elementary education (to age 14), and 40 percent proceed to the secondary level. The adult literacy rate is 84 percent, and there are hundreds of higher-education institutions.

Language. Portuguese is Brazil's official language, differing slightly from the pronunciation spoken in Portugal. English and French are popular second languages, and Spanish is becoming popular as Brazil establishes stronger trade ties with its neighbors.

Customs and Courtesies. In formal situations, Brazilians greet each other with a handshake. Friends embrace and kiss each other on alternating cheeks, although they may only touch cheeks and "kiss the air." A common greeting is "Ola. Tudo bem?" (Hello. Is everything fine?) or "Como vai?" (How are you?). "Senhor"(Mr.) or "senhora" (Mrs.) are the formal titles that precede surnames. Gestures are commonly used to express feelings: pulling one eyelid down signifies disbelief or caution, tapping the fingers horizontally under the chin indicates that another person does not know what he or she is talking about, and the U.S. American "okay" sign, with the thumb and index finger forming a circle, is an offensive gesture.

Appearance. Brazilians are fashionable and enjoy European (and particularly Italian) styles of clothing. People in warm and humid climates dress more casually, and colors are lighter and brighter. In the south, including São Paulo, people more often dress in black, white, and other neutral colors.

Families. Families are large and may include the extended family, although smaller families of up to three children are becoming more common. The family is led by the father, but the mother influences decisions, especially those affecting the home. Generally, women are responsible for household duties even if they work outside the home. Children rarely leave home before they marry, and the elderly who cannot care for themselves live with their children.

Recreation. The people of Brazil have a passion for soccer (futebol), so much so that schools and businesses close during the World Cup games. Basketball and volleyball are also popular, and many Brazilians are avid fans of auto racing. People commonly watch television, especially soap operas (telenovelas). Traditional festivals are popular, and Brazilians celebrate many occasions with singing and samba dancing.

Food. Breakfast usually consists of coffee with milk (café com leite), fruit, and bread with marmalade. Lunch is the main meal and often includes beans, rice, meat, salad, potatoes, bread, and fruit. Dinner is lighter, consisting of a bowl of soup with bread, followed by a piece of cake. In Bahia, foods may be spiced with palm (dendé) oil. Churrasco, which originated in the south, is a barbecue with a variety of meats.

Holidays. The single most important holiday of Brazil is Carnaval, a five-day festival preceding Ash Wednesday. It is marked by street parades, samba dancing, parties, drinking, costumes, drumming, and music. Tiradentes Day (April 21) celebrates the death of Joaquim José da Silva Xavier (known as Tiradentes), a dentist and a nationalist who died in the struggle for independence. The Festas Juninas (June Festivals) coincides with the feasts of St. John and St. Peter. Other festivals include Easter, Independence Day (September 7), Memorial Day (November 2), and Republic Day (November 15). Christmas Eve is an occasion for the family to gather for a meal (turkey or ham) and gift exchange; the gifts from Papai Noel (Father Noel) arrive Christmas Day. New Year's Eve is a time for parties. Candomblé believers dress in white and blue to honor the sea goddess Lemanjá and gain energy for the new year.

Bambu
(Bamboo Tree)

About the Song

Brazil's music has influenced jazz and popular musicians throughout the world. Upon hearing it, people from the Netherlands to Nigeria have been known to go into a dancing frenzy! Children in Brazil grow up with the sounds of samba and bossa nova in their ears and are at home with rhythmically sophisticated music in their early years. In addition to the adult music that surrounds them, Brazilian children also learn to sing children's songs from adults, older siblings, and other children. "Bambu" is one of those songs in which children are playfully assimilated into Brazilian culture—its language, rhythms, and melodies. The children of Teca Oficina de Música, directed by Teca Alencar de Brito, sing "Bambu," one of a set of 28 songs from a recording called *Cantos de Vários Cantos*. The children range in age from six to eight years, and they are accompanied by guitar, accordian, zabumba (bass drum), and a variety of hand-held percussion instruments ⑮ .

Bambu

Brazil

Bambu, tirabu,
Bahm-boo chee-dah-boo

Aroeira, mantegueira.
Ah-doo-ay-dah mahn-teh-gay-dah

Tirara a Luiza,
Chee-da-dah ah Loo-ee-zah

Para ser bambu.
Pah-dah zehd bahm-boo

Text in English

Bamboo, tirabu (a playful expression)
Aroeira, mantegueira (two types of Brazilian trees)
They took Luiza
To become a bamboo tree.

Teaching Suggestions

1. Locate Brazil on a map of South America, and note its size in relation to other countries on the continent. See that it covers half the area of the South American continent. Locate the Amazon River, the second largest in the world (after the Nile), and some of the cities of Brazil: Rio de Janeiro, Brasília (the capital), Bahia, and São Paulo.

2. Discuss the varied climates of Brazil and the varied animal and plant life found there. Find and list the types of animals, plants, and trees that grow in the tropical forests of the north, the broad Mato Grosso plains of the central and western regions, the coastal area, and the more temperate climate of the south. Encourage students to determine the prevalence of bamboo, aroeira, and mantegueira trees in northeastern Brazil, where this song originated, where indigenous people emphasized the elements of nature in their rituals, stories, and songs.

3. Listen to the recording of "Bambu," and listen for the word "bambu" at the beginning and end of each verse.

4. Through several listenings of the song, challenge students to (a) hear other "words" (or phonemes), (b) identify the instruments that accompany the singers, (c) keep the pulse by patting on "1" and clapping on "2," and (d) follow the pitches of the melody, raising and lowering hands to show the contour of the melody.

5. Learn to sing the song. Sing on a neutral syllable like "doo," on solfège syllables, and then with the Portuguese words. Note that in the third line, the names of children can vary from "Luiza" to "Julia" to any child's name. Use names from your class.

6. Play the accompaniment to the song on pitched and unpitched percussion instruments. Alternate singers and players of these instruments.

7. In a game that corresponds to the song, have players stand in a circle while one designated as It steps along the inside of the circle. On "tirara," It selects a player and the two join hands and dance in the circle. When there are two Its, the more recently selected It selects a new player and the three of them join hands to dance. To make the game work logistically, the verse should be sung twice: the first time around, the third line is sung without the name of a person ("tirara"—and then hum while It selects someone) and the second time, the third line is sung with the name of the newly selected person ("tirara a Rachel" or "tirara a Andrew," for example).

8. Encourage the discovery of Brazil. Look into its varied regional climates, flora and fauna, and the music that is derived from these regions. (Editor's note: You can go to any search engine on the Web and search for "Brazil"; many search engines allow you to search for sites with photographs.)

Bambu

Classroom Instrumental Arrangement

Brazil

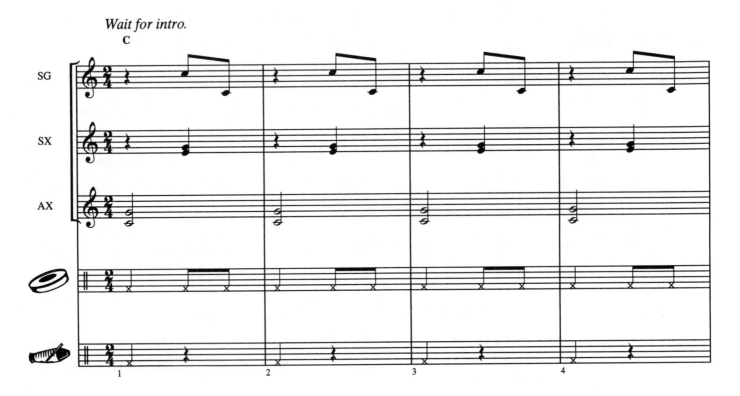

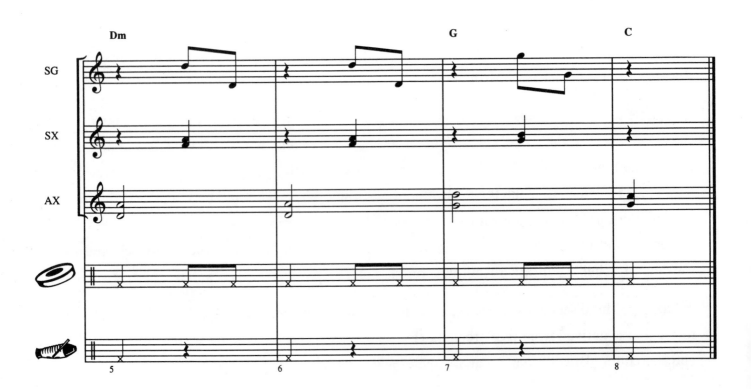

0562B

Cajueiro Pequenino
(The Little Cashew Tree)

About the Song

What were the sources of inspiration for the musical brilliance of Milton Nascimento, Gilberto Gil, Clara Nunes, Martinho da Vila, Tom (Antonio Carlos) Jobim, and João Gilberto? What were these musicians' musical roots that sent them onward to their performances of samba, choro, bossa nova, and other distinctively Brazilian sounds? As children, they might have been singing songs like "Cajueiro Pequenino," a straightforward melody enriched by the rhythmic and percussive layers that accompany it. The amazing rhythmic dynamism of Brazilian music is evident in all of its forms, including this song sung by children. Teca Alecar de Brito's group, Teca Oficina de Música, sings "Cajueiro Pequenino." The lead singer, Gabriela, is joined by a group of seven singers in imitation of the melody. Instruments include guitar, accordion, zabumba (bass drum), panderio (small hand drums), bongos, and triangle ⓖ .

Cajueiro Pequenino

Brazil

A *Wait for intro.*
Verse 1:

Ca - ju - ei - ro pe - que - ni - no ca - rre - ga - do de fu - ló. Eu tam -

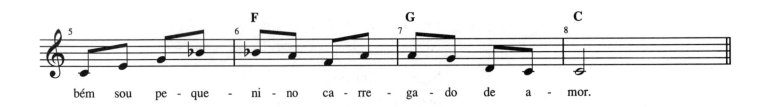

bém sou pe - que - ni - no ca - rre - ga - do de a - mor.

B *Verse 2:*

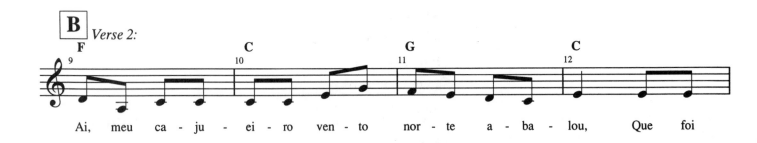

Ai, meu ca - ju - ei - ro ven - to nor - te a - ba - lou, Que foi

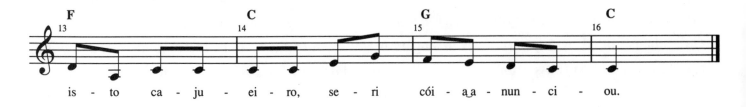

is - to ca - ju - ei - ro, se - ri có - i - a a - nun - ci - ou.

The Song Text

Verse 1:

Cajueiro pequenino

Kah-zhoo-eh-doh peh-kay-nee-noh

Carregado de fulô.

Kah-deh-gah-doh jee foo-loh

Eu tambem sou pequenino

Eo tahm-behm soh peh-kay-nee-noh

Carregado de amor.

Kah-deh-gah-doh jee ah-mohd

Verse 2:

Ai, meu cajueiro

Ah, meh kah-zhoo-eh-doh

Vento norte abalou,

Ben-to nohd-chee ah-bah-loh

Que foi isto cajueiro,

Keh foy ees-toh kah-zhoo-eh-doh

Sericoia anunciou.

Seh-dee-coh-yah-noon-see-oh

Text in English

Verse 1:

My little cashew tree
Filled with life
I am little, too.
And filled with love.

Verse 2:

Oh, my little cashew tree
That the north wind shook
Oh, what was that about?
The story the bird told.

Teaching Suggestions

1. Refer to Teaching Suggestions 1 and 2 from "Bambu" in setting the geographic and cultural context of "Cajueira Pequenino." Note the element of nature that is featured in this children's song: the cashew tree (just as "Bambu" features other Brazilian trees).

2. While listening to the song, pat-clap-tap the rhythm: ♪. ♩ ♩ . Feel it that way and also with a tie between the sixteenth and quarter (although this is a more sophisticated rhythm to feel and play): ♪. ♩♩ . Try several rhythms at once: clap (or play maracas) on the beat, pat (or play djembe drum) on ♪. ♩ ♩ , and pat (or play conga drum) on ♩ ♪♪♪♪ . Play the pattern on a low pitch for the first quarter note and use a higher sound for the four sixteenths.

3. Listen for the different sound of Portuguese and compare it to the Spanish that is spoken in the surrounding Latin American countries. Note the sound of *de* as "jee," with the English "j" sound.

4. Listen to the solo voice on recording, and, like the children on the recording, sing verse 1 in imitation. At first, perhaps only a few words (or syllables) will be sung correctly, but through repeated listenings, the sounds will begin to gel in the ears and voices of singers. Omitting the recording, slow down the melody and instruct children to sing softly so they can better hear each syllable.

5. Plan the instrumental accompaniment on alto and soprano xylophones, along with the unpitched rhythmic ostinati on maracas, bass djembe, and conga drums. Another plan is to play one of the drum rhythms on hand drums, making the sound of the Brazilian pandeiro.

6. Select the music of Milton Nascimento, Gilberto Gil, Clara Nunes, Martinho da Vila, Tom (Antonio Carlos) Jobim, and João Gilberto for extended listening. Consider that these musicians may have once sung "Cajueiro Pequenino." Ask in what ways this little children's song might have laid the "roots" for these famous singers' musical development.

Cajueiro Pequenino

Classroom Instrumental Arrangement

Brazil

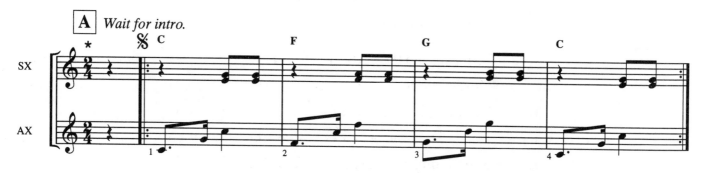

All measures ostinati
(play same pattern throughout)

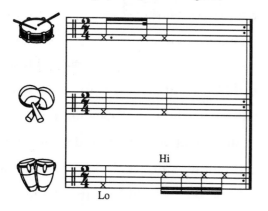

*The rhythms may be taught in $\frac{4}{4}$ to simplify, so that $\sqcap$ $\sqcap$ = $\lrcorner$. $\flat$

Chile

The musical and artistic expressions of Chile have been either overlooked or underestimated by far too many whose mission is a broad and encompassing understanding of the world's cultures for themselves and their students. To do so is to miss the children's songs present there, the nueva canción (songs of protest against totalitarian oppression or foreign cultural interference), and also the tonada, the quintessential song of Chile for guitar (or harp and guitar, or rebec and guitar) and, traditionally, feminine voice. Tucked away on the southwestern coast of South America, Chile seems to hide in the shadow of the Andes mountains that run all the way to the southern tip of the continent. Yet there is a lively Chilean culture, and multiple cultures residing within Chile, that can be observed in Santiago, the capital city, and also in the mountain villages as well as the high deserts of the north. Chileans sing their songs with passion, whether of romance or political protest, and for those who take the time to listen, the Chilean spirit is revealed to them.

The Musical Surroundings: Getting to Know Chile

Land and People. The average width of Chile, the "Shoestring Country," is just 110 miles, although it stretches more than 2,600 miles from north to south. The Incas arrived first in Chile in the mid-fifteenth century, finding indigenous cultures such as the Mapuche (who constitute three percent of the population today, along with another two percent of other indigenous peoples). Like many other Latin American countries, the region was conquered by the Spanish in 1536 and spent several centuries under their rule until independence was accomplished in 1817 through the efforts of Chilean patriots who joined with the armies of liberator José de San Martín. Unstable governments and military interventions dot Chilean history and include attempts at socialism through Marxist rule by Salvador Allende in the early 1970s, followed by the authoritarian leader General Augusto Pinochet Ugarte, and more recently a more democratic view of socialism. About 95 percent of Chileans are either of European heritage or mestizo (mixed European-indigenous descent). Chile has been referred to as the "Switzerland of the Andes" for its natural beauty: lakes, forests, volcanoes, and a wide variety of plants and animals.

Economy. Chile's economy is prosperous and growing, and Chileans enjoy access to health care and education (although the disparity between men's and women's wages is considerable). The country is one of the world's largest producers of copper, and it includes copper along with grapes, apples, nectarines, and peaches among its chief exports. Agriculture, fish, metals, and wood products are important to its economy.

Education. Schooling is free and compulsory for children between the ages of five and seventeen, and through public and private schooling Chile has one of the best-educated populations in Latin America. Its adult literacy rate is 95 percent.

Language. Spanish, called Castellano, is the official language of Chile. Chileans commonly add a suffix (*-ito*) to words and names to form diminutives: *chaolito* is a "small goodbye" and Carlito means "little Carlos." English is taught in the schools, and small minority groups also speak German (in southern Chile) and Mapuche.

Customs and Courtesies. The abrazo, a handshake and hug, supplemented with a kiss to the right cheek for women and family members, is the most common greeting. Eye contact is essential during conversation, as is correct posture. Traditional verbal greetings include: "¿Qué tal?" (What's going on?), "¿Cómo estai?" (informal for How are you?), "Gusto de verte!" (Nice to see you), and "¿Quí hubo?" (What's up?). Chileans, more than other Latin Americans, address others with the formal "usted" (you) more often than with the familiar "tú." Titles such as "señor" (Mr.), "señora" (Mrs.), "señorita" (Miss), and professional titles (doctor, director, professor) are used. Yawns are suppressed or politely concealed with the hand. Items, including money, are handed, never tossed, to others. Chileans point with puckered lips rather than with the index finger.

Appearance. In urban areas, fashions are sophisticated and European in style. U.S. American casual fashions are popular among youth. Many commercial entities such as banks and department stores require their employees to wear uniforms. Sloppy or tattered clothing is considered poor taste, even for lower-income people and even in rural areas.

Families. The extended family is important to Chileans, so that children are frequently living with parents and grandparents. A change in the attitudes about women in the professional world has occurred in recent years, so that women are now 30 percent of the labor force. Reciprocity characterizes the relationship between husband and wife, with the man performing courtesies for the woman and vice versa. It is customary for a person to bear two family names: the last name is the mother's family name and the second-to-last name is the father's family name. People use either their full name or go by their father's family name, which is the official surname. As in other Latin American countries, women retain their father's family name rather than use that of their husbands.

Recreation. Soccer (fútbol) is the most popular sport, and basketball is gaining in popularity. Chileans enjoy swimming, going to parks, and watching videos at home. Vacations to the coast or the countryside are common during holidays. Rodeo is popular in many areas, with cowboys (huasos) wearing handwoven capes and straw hats.

Food. Chileans eat their main meal at noon and a light meal between 8 p.m. and 10 p.m. Afternoon tea (onces) with small sandwiches and pastries is also customary. They enjoy empanadas de horno (meat turnovers with beef and hard-boiled eggs), pastel de choclo (a baked meal of beef, chicken, onions, corn, eggs, and spices), cazuela de ave (chicken soup), and seafood casseroles. Children enjoy eating sopapillas made from a deep-fried pumpkin dough sprinkled with sugar.

Holidays. Chileans celebrate New Year's Day, Easter, National Day (September 11), Armed Forces Day (September 19), All Saints Day (November 1), and Christmas. On Independence Day, people go to parks and eat empanadas, drink chicha (a drink of fermented grapes), and dance the cueca (the national dance) to guitar music. Many families hold outdoor barbecues on Christmas Eve and open their gifts at midnight.

El Rabel
(The Violin)

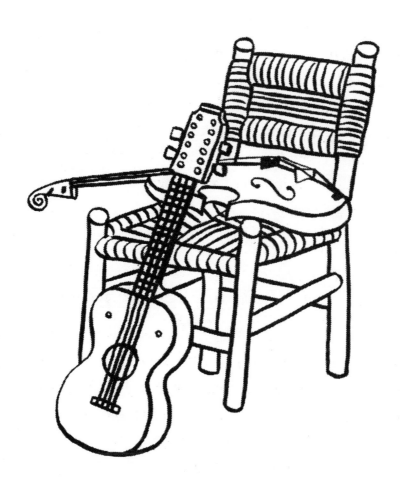

About the Song

Given the international attention to the Chilean protest song known as nueva canción, as well as the artful tonada, one might be led to believe that there are no "regular" folk songs in Chile that are not linked to political expressions, religious beliefs, or musical structures emanating from those found in Renaissance Europe. But adults and children alike sing songs of the Chilean landscape, of work and play, of festive occasions, and of reasons to make music and dance.

Mireya Alegría of Santiago, Chile, sings "El Rabel" 🌐 from the Zona de Chiloe, a region in the southern part of the country that was the last Hispanic bastion on the South American continent and thus a repository of Hispanic traditions. Even today, popular Renaissance dances originating from central Spain persist there. No doubt, the song text refers to just this type of dancing, complete with the twirling of a silk handkerchief and sung to the accompaniment of stringed instruments.

El Rabel

Chile

El ra - bel pa - ra ser fi - no ha de ser de ver - de pi - no, la

vi - hue - la d(e) du - ra he - bra y el se - dal de mu - la ne - gra, la

vi - hue - la d(e) du - ra he - bra y el se - dal de mu - la ne - gra.

An - da mo - re - ni - ta re - co - je e - se pa - ñue - lo.

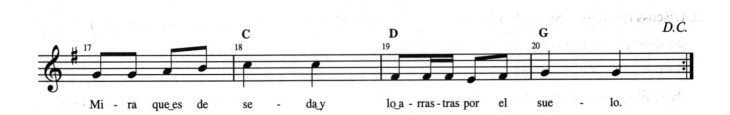

Mi - ra que es de se - da y lo a - rras - tras por el sue - lo.

The Song Text

El rabel para ser fino ha de ser de verde pino

Ehl rah-behl pah-rah sehr fee-no ah deh sehr deh vehr-day spee-noh

La vihuela de dura hebra y el sedal de mula negra

Lah vee-hway-lahd doo-rah eh-brah yehl say-dahl deh moo-lah neh-grah

La vihuela de dura hebra ye el sedal de mula negra

Lah vee-hway-lahd doo-rah eh-brah yehl say-dahl deh moo-lah neh-grah

Anda morenita recoge ese pañuelo.

Ahn-dah moh-reh-nee-tah reh-koh-yeh-say pahn-way-loh

Mira que es de seda y lo arrastras por el suelo. *(repeat last two lines)*
Mee-rah kays deh say-dah ee loah-rahs-trahs pohr ehl sway-loh..

Text in English

The finest violin is made of (the wood of) the green pine tree,

The vihuela (a guitar-like instrument) is made of hard wood,

With its strings made of the hair of a black mule.

Come, little girl (of tanned/brown skin),

Pick up the handkerchief.

See that it is made of silk as you drag it across the floor.

(The English translation of a second verse, neither transliterated nor found in the recorded children's performance, is given here.)
Give a hug to that girl who is dancing.

Pat the back of the young man who goes to dance with her.

Teaching Suggestions

1. Look for the location of Chile, and comment on the size and shape that has warranted the expression "the Shoestring Country." Discover on a topographical map the mountains and valleys, the coastal areas, the northern desert, the scarcely populated region of the far south that breaks into numerous island groups, and, of course, the capital city of Santiago.

2. Discuss the strong Spanish influence in Chile, sparked by this information: (a) the Spanish arrived and conquered the region in 1536, (b) 95 percent of the population is either of European (mostly Spanish) heritage or mestizo, (c) Spanish remains the official language, and (d) there are regions such as Zona de Chiloe so insular that cultural expressions of the Spanish Renaissance remain nearly unchanged!

3. Listen to the recording of "El Rabel," and follow the strumming rhythm of the guitar by tapping on laps, desktops, or floors.

4. Identify some of the words within the song verse, pronouncing them and writing them: "rabel" (violin), "vihuela" (vihuela lute, guitar-like instrument), "mula negra" (black mule), "anda" (come), and "mira" (see).

5. Listen for these words in the song, and follow them in print to see how they fit into the text. Explain that the song describes musical instruments (and the materials of which they are made) and the dance they accompany.

6. Learn to sing the song, adding the unpitched percussion instruments (a conga's high and low timbre) and the woodblock with the guitar strum.

7. Play the soprano and alto xylophone accompaniment along with the conga and woodblock, alone and then while singing. Experiment with singing the song with xylophones and then with guitar, retaining conga and woodblock in either case, and discuss the different mood these instruments create.

8. Perform a circle dance that coincides to four-measure, eight-beat phrases. Have all students hold hands, with a small handkerchief or scarf in the right hand (or tied to the right wrist). Count off "ones" and "twos" so that every other "player" can move in one of two sections at the end ("ones" on measures 7–20 and "twos" on measures 21–24). Begin with arms down, separated, and facing inward to the center of the circle.

   Measures 1–4: All turn around to the right, arriving back and facing in to the center of the circle on beat 8 and in place; while turning, twirl the scarves with right hands above the heads.

   Measures 5–8: All turn right, stepping eight times to the right.

   Measures 9–12: All turn left, stepping eight times to the left.

   Measures 13–16: All "ones" step eight steps forward into the center of the circle.

   Measures 17–20: All "twos" take eight steps forward to center of the circle.

9. Extend the Chilean musical experience by exploring the music of nueva canción singers like Víctor Jara, Violeta Parra, Quilapayún, and Inti Illimani.

El Rabel

Classroom Instrumental Arrangement

Chile

All measures ostinati
(play same pattern throughout)

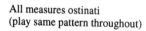

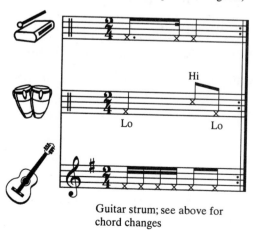

Guitar strum; see above for
chord changes

Cuba

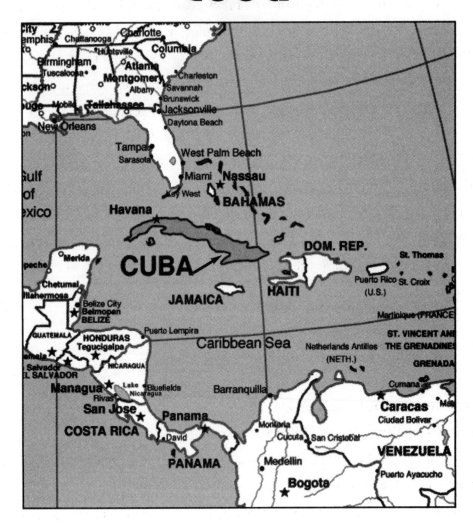

It took the Buena Vista Social Club's world-beat recordings and the 1998 film of the same name to bring the music of Cuba to the world's ears, and as a result the floodgates have opened wide for exchange both in and out of Cuba. Cuban musicians are recording and touring in unprecedented numbers; travel to Cuba by Latin Americans, Europeans, and North Americans has increased dramatically; and outsiders are developing an awareness of not only the music of Cuba, but also the culture that spawns it. Lying just 90 miles south of the United States, Cuba and its musical culture are ripe for "discovery," and its music and dance forms, including the rhumba, the mambo, the guaguancó, and even Cuban-style salsa are undergoing a sort of renewed interest at home and abroad. These days, "Cubanismo" is *de rigeur* for adults and children—Cubans and non-Cubans alike.

The Musical Surroundings: Getting to Know Cuba

Land and People. Cuba is an archipelago of two main islands, Cuba and Isla de la Juventud (Isle of Youth), and about 1,600 keys and islets. Cuba was inhabited by three indigenous groups, principally the Taíno, prior to the arrival of Christopher Columbus in 1492. By 1532, the enslaved Native population had been wiped out by the Spanish colony that had been established just 21 years earlier. Africans were brought to Cuba to work as slaves on the sugar plantations in the eighteenth and nineteenth centuries. Cuba remained in Spanish hands far longer than most other Latin American countries, despite uprisings, including one in 1895 led by José Martí, Cuba's national hero. Spain's treatment of Cuba led to U.S. involvement in the Spanish-American War of 1898, after which Cuba gained independence. A military coup in 1952 established a dictatorship under General Fulgencio Batista, which was overthrown in 1959 by a rebel movement under the leadership of Fidel Castro. Cuba enjoyed support in the communist world through the 1980s, and although the U.S. broke off relations with the country, Castro's socialist development brought about agrarian reform, nationalization of industry, and the creation of rural cooperatives. Today, three-quarters of the people live in urban areas like Havana, the capital city. The population is two-thirds Spanish origin, 12 percent black African ancestry, and about 22 percent mixed origin. Just to the north, more than one million Cuban-Americans live in Florida (in the U.S.).

Economy. Free markets for crafts and produce have opened since the Soviet block dissolved in the early 1990s, while self-employment and joint ventures with foreign firms were seen for the first time in more than three decades. Agriculture employs about 20 percent of the labor force, with main crops like sugarcane, tobacco, citrus fruit, coffee, and rice. Many Cuban-Americans send money and gifts to their families in Cuba, which allows about half of all Cubans access to goods not otherwise available in the country.

Education. Cubans prioritize education for children, and the state provides free primary, secondary, technical, and higher education to all citizens. More than 90 percent of all children continue with secondary education, and the adult literacy rate is 96 percent.

Language. Spanish is Cuba's official language, with slight accent and pronunciation differences across the country's three regions. Many words are unique to Cuban society, such as *pelotear* (to pass the buck), *plan jaba* (a special shopping plan for working women), *amarillo* (traffic official), and *rebambaramba* (a free-for-all). English is a required course in secondary schools.

Customs and Courtesies. Men greet with a handshake and "¿Qué tal?" (How are you?). Most women kiss each other once on the cheek for hello. People usually address others by first name, and strangers frequently use "compañero" or "compañera" (comrade) to address one another. Cubans are lively in conversation, using hand gestures to reinforce ideas. It is not considered rude to interrupt a friend during conversation, and people often touch and tap each other to make a point. One beckons by waving fingers inward with the palm down.

Appearance. People wear lightweight, casual clothing. Women of all ages wear slacks, jeans, short skirts, blouses, and canvas shoes or sandals, reserving dresses only for more formal occasions. Men wear long pants, jeans, and shirts or t-shirts; formal wear features a guayabera, a traditional square-cut shirt. Schoolchildren wear uniforms.

Families. Cubans maintain strong family ties, so many households include grandparents. When adult children marry, they usually live with parents until they can obtain housing, which is in short supply. Women account for 37 percent of the workforce and 55 percent of the country's specialists. Still, they are responsible for most household chores and child care. As in Chile (and other Latin American countries), a person bears two family names: the last is the mother's family name, and the second-to-last is the name of the father's family.

Recreation. Sports are highly developed in Cuba, and the country shows well in the Olympic games. The most popular sport is baseball, and boys begin playing in leagues by the age of seven. Girls enjoy sports in school, but women do not usually play baseball. Dominoes is a national pastime played by males of all ages (especially retired men). Dancing is common at discos, festivals, and family parties.

Food. A light desayuno (breakfast) consists of a cup of black coffee. Most workers eat almuerzo (lunch) at work or school, and the family gets together in the evening for comida (dinner). The Cuban diet is based on foods grown locally. Arroz y frijoles (rice and beans) is the traditional staple meal. Eggs are eaten boiled, fried, and as omelettes, and corn is the basis of many foods. Tropical fruits are common, including mangoes, guavas, oranges, lemons, pineapples, and papayas.

Holidays. Liberation Day (January 1) commemorates the revolution of 1958 and 1959, preceded by New Year's Eve (December 31). Other holidays are the Anniversary of the Attack on the Moncada Garrison in Santiago de Cuba in 1953 (July 26), the Beginning of the War of Independence from Spain (October 10), and Mother's Day (the second Sunday of May). Religious holidays are not officially recognized but are often celebrated with feasts and religious services, including Christmas, Holy Week, and Easter. Some holidays honor deities of the Catholic religion and of Santería (a religion that combines ideas of African origin with Catholicism), for example, the feast of St. Barbara and the African goddess Changó on December 4.

Ma Teodora
(Mother Teodora)

About the Song

Work songs, lullabies, topical songs, sea shanteys, music for stick-fighting, improvised poetry contests, and ensembles consisting of guitars and various percussion instruments make up the musical expressions of people in Cuba and throughout the Caribbean. There are Afro-Cuban drumming groups of congas and claves, often joined by guitars and brass instruments, that provide richly textured polyrhythms for dancing in clubs, in community centers, and on festive occasions just about anywhere else. There are also folk songs, songs that are passed on orally, whose melodies contain a rare rhythmic vitality. "Ma Teodora" represents just that type of song: traditional, orally transmitted, and with rhythmic interest embedded in the melody.

The singer and musicians ⏻ offer just enough of a saucy rhythm to pique the interest of listeners to entice them to join in singing, and possibly playing and dancing as well.

Ma Teodora

Cuba

¿Dón - de es - tá la Ma Teo - do - ra?___ Ra - jan - do la le - ña es -

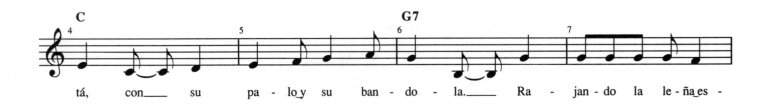

tá, con___ su pa - lo y su ban - do - la.___ Ra - jan - do la le - ña es -

tá. ¿Dón - de es - tá que no la ve - o?___ Ra - jan - do la le - ña es -

tá. Ra - jan - do la le - ña es - tá. Ra - jan - do la le - ña es - tá.

The Song Text

¿Dónde está la Ma Teodora?
Dohn-days-tah lah Mah Tay-oh-doh-rah

Rajando la leña está.
Rah-hahn-doh lah lay-nyahs-tah

Con su palo y su bandola.
Kohn soo pah-loy soo bahn-doh-lah

Rajando la leña está.
Rah-hahn-doh lah lay-nyahs-tah

¿Dónde está que no la veo?
Dohn-days-tah kay noh lah vay-oh

Rajando la leña está. *(sing three times)*
Rah-hahn-doh lah lay-nyahs-tah

Text in English

Where is Mother Teodora?
She's cutting the firewood
With her pole and her bandola (lute-like instrument).
She's cutting the firewood.
Why can't we see her?
She's cutting the firewood. *(sing three times)*

Teaching Suggestions

1. **Several perspectives of Cuba are necessary to tell the stories of this island country, one of which is a map that shows Cuba's place in the Caribbean, its proximity to North America (Florida, in the U.S.), Mexico, and South America. Also, a close-up of Cuba will reveal the urban industrialized areas and the vast spread of farmlands for growing sugarcane, tobacco, and other warm-weather crops. Trace the distance between Cuba and Florida, and comment on the large Cuban-American population in Florida that continues to keep strong connections with family members on the island.**

2. **Discuss the socialist view of government of Cuba, which created rural cooperative communities and a reform and strengthening of agrarian ways. Note that despite the growth of industries and manufacturing in Cuba, there is still a strong leaning toward continuing farming practices and craft-making tra-**

ditions, which is more prominent in Cuba than in most other Latin American countries.

3. Listen to the recording of "Ma Teodora," and challenge students to follow the quick 6/8 pulse. Does it always sound the same, or does it seem to change? Draw attention to the sesquiáltera (changing sixes) that divide between a feeling of twos and threes. Lead students in tapping or patting the two-pattern and then the three-pattern. Once mastered, try having some students pat the two-pattern repeatedly while others pat the three-pattern over and over again. After each group of six beats, everyone should be together on beat 1. Relate this exercise to multiplying 2 x 3 or 3 x 2 to equal six. Emphasize the beat shown in bold: (2) **1** 2 **1** 2 **1** 2   or   **1** 2 3 4 5 6

          (3) **1** 2 3 **1** 2 3   or   **1** 2 3 4 5 6

4. Learn to ask the question, "¿Dónde está Ma Teodora?" (Where is Ma Teodora?), substituting the names of people and places for "Ma Teodora." Learn also a response: "Ma Teodora (or substitute name of person or place) está aquí" (Ma Teodora is here) or "Ma Teodora (or substitute) está allí" (Ma Teodora is there). Share the translation of the song, and suggest that the mention of the word "bandola" might suggest that even as the woman labors to cut wood, she takes an occasional musical break to play her instrument.

5. Learn to sing the song, both without and then with patting the pulse (as in #3). Changing from the feeling of two to the feeling of three is not easy! Sing it at different tempos to discover the various feelings of the pulse. This will make a nice transition to performing the accompanying parts on unpitched and pitched percussion instruments.

6. Play the pitched percussion accompaniment on xylophones, adding also the cowbell, guiro, and drum. The accompaniment can be played alone as well as with singers on the melody. Consider a performance in which the piece is performed five times as on 🔊 , with instrumental (i) and instrument-with-voice (iv) versions alternating: i, iv, i, iv, i.

7. Try a basic dance step on the accented pulses, stepping two or three times per measure. In a single line with one dancer behind the next (arms bent at elbows and hands in loose fists), move the stepping pattern forward similar to the old-fashioned conga line.

8. For a more extended study of Cuban music, listen to Celina González, Cuba's "Queen of Country Music" and Cuban exile Celia Cruz, the "Queen of New York Salsa." Pay attention to sounds of the rhumba, danzón, chachachá, mambo, son, and salsa in dozens of recently released recordings, and listen for the claves, the guagua (wooden tube played with sticks), and conga drums—all demonstrative of African influences.

Ma Teodora

Classroom Instrumental Arrangement

Cuba

Guatemala

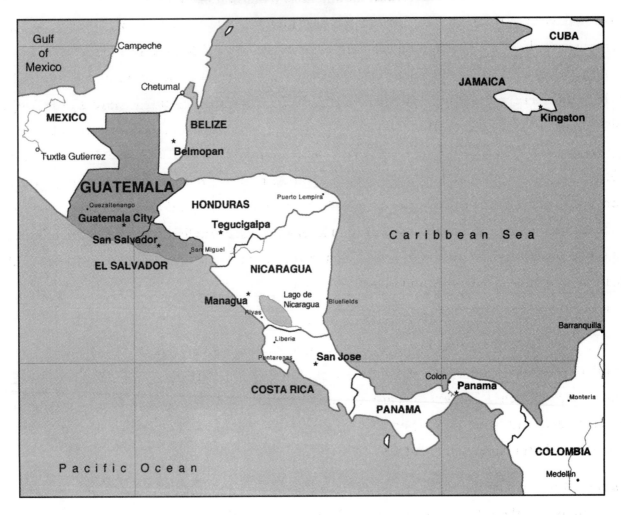

At any time of the day or night, there is probably someone in Guatemala playing a marimba. For those who love the sound of the marimba, Guatemala is the place to be; it's the ultimate marimba kingdom! Marimbas are like xylophones: both have wooden bars, but the marimba's tone is enhanced and amplified by the resonance chambers that hang below each bar. A history of the Guatemalan marimba is a study of the social fabric of the nation. Brought by Africans to their Caribbean coastal communities in the late 1600s, the marimba was adopted by the indigenous peoples as their melody instrument and then further acculturated by the Spanish ruling class. Whether on the slopes of the highlands or in the well-watered lowlands along the Pacific coast, whether at a family party or at one of the many annual festivals, marimbas are played solo and in ensemble to accompany songs, and as música pura, the "pure" music of Guatemala, untampered, unblended.

The Musical Surroundings: Getting to Know Guatemala

Land and People. Guatemala is a mountainous country where volcanoes are active and the tremors of earthquakes are frequent. The Mayan Empire flourished for more than a thousand years in Guatemala, and there are archaeological ruins to prove it. From 1524 until its independence in 1821, Guatemala was ruled by Spain. This was followed by a period of annexation and rule by Mexico. From 1838 until a revolution in 1944, the country was controlled by military dictatorships. Coups and civil war made for political instability until 1996, when the two sides made peace with each other following the loss of 150,000 lives. There is common agreement to downsize the military, to attend to indigenous people's rights, and to work toward agrarian reform. Of 12 million Guatemalans, 56 percent are ladino or mestizo (mixed blood), and 44 percent are composed of some 28 groups descended from the Maya who refer to themselves as indígenas. A small English-speaking black minority, the Garífuna, is found on the Caribbean coast. High in the mountains and in the hot, humid coastal lowlands, there is relative peace now in Guatemala; it's a time to enjoy the treasures of the "Land of the Eternal Spring."

Economy. Guatemala is relatively poor, with three-quarters of its rural residences and two-thirds of its urban inhabitants living in poverty. About 60 percent of the people are employed in agriculture. Coffee accounts for 25 percent of all export earnings, and other leading products include cotton, cacao, corn, beans, sugarcane, and bananas. Women earn roughly one-fifth of the nation's income, the lowest proportion among Latin American countries.

Education. More than half of primary-age children do not attend school. Literacy is higher for men and urban dwellers, but the rate for them is only 67 percent. In rural areas, children do not speak Spanish, the language of instruction. They still speak languages of the indígenas, primarily Cakchiquel. Facilities are often crowded, books are in short supply, and teachers are underpaid.

Language. Spanish is Guatemala's official language. Although most male indigenous Guatemalans also speak some Spanish, indigenous women have fewer opportunities to attend school and therefore do not learn Spanish.

Customs and Courtesies. When meeting for the first time, people greet with a handshake and "Mucho gusto" (Pleased to meet you). Among friends, men usually shake hands and sometimes embrace, and ladino women kiss each other on the cheek. Some older women greet by grasping each other just below each elbow. In small groups, it is important to greet each individual. Guatemalans beckon by waving the hand downward and in. A "tsst tsst" sound gets someone's attention. Pointing with the finger or hand can be misinterpreted because many finger and hand gestures are considered vulgar.

Appearance. People wear Western-style clothing in cities. Most rural Maya, particularly women, have retained traditional dress. Basic features include a faja (woven belt worn by both sexes), a corte (wraparound skirt) for women, and knee- or calf-length trousers for men. Women may weave ribbons through their hair, and men generally wear hats made of straw or blocked felt. A woman treasures her huipil (blouse): its design identifies her status and hometown.

Families. The extended family forms the basis of society. The father is the head of the family, but the mother controls the household; she is considered the heart of the family. Rural extended families often share a single home or live next to each other in a family compound that includes parents, married sons and their families, unmarried children, and often grandparents. Urban families generally live in nuclear family settings, although grandparents are often present. One-fourth of the labor force is female, and ladino women work as secretaries, teachers, and nurses. In poor families, children must work as soon as they can to help support the family.

Recreation. Popular sports include soccer, basketball, and volleyball, and family outings to a beach or lake are common holiday activities. Cofradías (religious fraternities dedicated to a particular saint) offer a variety of recreational and leisure activities. Visiting friends and relatives is the most common leisure activity among Guatemalans.

Food. Most people eat three meals a day, but poorer families might eat only one meal and then snack on tortillas the rest of the day. The main meal is eaten at midday. Corn tortillas or tamalitos (cornmeal dough wrapped in corn husks and steamed) are eaten with every meal. Other foods include black beans, rice, tamales, greens, and fried plátanos (bananas) with honey, cream, or black beans. Meats (beef, pork, and chicken) usually are stewed, and sauces are important. Guatemalans generally use utensils but may eat some foods with their hands or use tortillas as a scoop.

Holidays. Major celebrations are had at Christmas and Easter. Christmas season begins December 7, when people burn their garbage symbolically to rid their homes of evil. On Christmas Eve (Noche Buena), families set off firecrackers at midnight and then eat a large meal of tamales and hot chocolate. Easter is celebrated with Holy Week, during which numerous large processions fill the streets. National holidays include Army Day (June 30), Independence Day (September 15), Día de la Raza (Day of the Mestizo) Race or Columbus Day (October 12), Revolution Day (October 20), and All Saints' Day (November 1). Every rural town hosts an annual feria (fair) honoring the local patron saint.

Tamborcita
(The Little Drummer)

About the Song

We often remember not only the sights but also the sounds of our experiences. Conjure up the visual image of a little drummer standing by a small church in an up-country village in Guatemala, playing alongside the sounds of the church bells that toll at morning, noon, and six o'clock in the evening. Tapping away on the drum, the young drummer girl (or boy, tamborcito) plays along to the steady pulse of this song of childhood remembrances. Ethel Batris of Guatemala City, Guatemala, sings and plays "Tamborcita," while Rebeca Galindo provides a steady percussive ostinato throughout the song. Although this version gives a Hispanic (almost pan-Latin) feel to the song, the sound of wood xylophones in the arrangement recalls the marimbas that so uniquely distinguish the music of Guatemala 19.

Tamborcita

Guatemala

Wait for intro.
Verse 1:

Tam - bor - ci - ta de mi al - de - a nun - ca te ol - vi - da - ré

yo. So - nan - do des - de la i - gle - sia, so - nan - do el ron - co

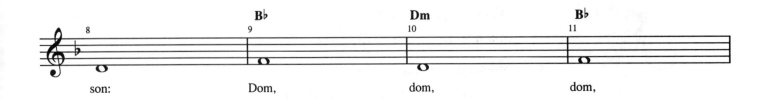

son: Dom, dom, dom,

Verse 2:

dom. Des - de el dí - a de San Pe - dro al de San Pas - cual, Bai -

lon al dí - a de San Eu - se - bio siem - pre so - nan - do tam -

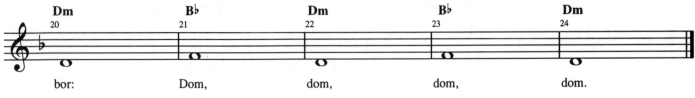

bor: Dom, dom, dom, dom.

0562B

58

The Song Text

Verse 1:

Tamborcita de mi aldea
Tam-bor-see-tah day mee ahl-day-ah

Nunca te olvidaré yo.
Noon-kah tay ol-vee-dah-ray yoe

Sonando desde la iglesia
Soh-nahn-doh des-day lah ee-glay-see-ah

Sonando el ronco son:
Soh-nahn-doh el rohn-koh son

Dom, dom, dom, dom.
Dohm dohm dohm dohm

Verse 2:

Desde el día de San Pedro
Dehs-day el dee-ah day Sahn Pay-droh

Al de San Pascual Bailón
Ahl day Sahn Pahs-kwal Bahy-lohn

Al día de San Eusebio
Ahl dee-ah day Sahn U-say-bee-oh

Siempre sonando tambor:
See-ehm-pray soh-nahn-doh tahm-bor

Dom, dom, dom, dom.
Dohm, dohm, dohm, dohm

Text in English

Verse 1:

Little drummer from my village,
I will never forget you
Sounding from the church,
Sounding the heavy bass sound:
Dom, dom, dom, dom.

Verse 2:

From the feastday of St. Peter
To the feastday of St. Pascal Bailon (patron of cooks)
To the feastday of St. Eusebius,
The drumming is always sounding: Dom, dom, dom, dom.

Teaching Suggestions

1. Draw students' attention to the map of Latin America, and challenge them to find Guatemala. If they are uncertain, offer clues such as "a country in Central America," "with both Pacific and Atlantic coast regions," or "a neighbor of Mexico." Look closer at Guatemala to find its capital city of Ciudad de Guatemala, its large lakes (Lago de Izabal, Lago de Atitlán), and the influence of indigenous peoples on the names of many of its cities and towns (Quezaltenango, Mazatenango, Totonicapán, for example).

2. Describe the traditional life of many Guatemalans (and other Latin Americans as well, particularly in towns and villages) that centers around the church in the plaza and on the celebration of the feastdays (usually birthdays) of saints. Note that three religious figures, or saints, are remembered by the singer: St. Peter, St. Pascal Bailon, and St. Eusebius. Discuss the manner in which major feastdays are celebrated: church services in the morning, families together for meals, music and dancing in the evenings in the plaza.

3. Listen to the recording of "Tamborcita." Challenge students to identify how the singer describes the sound of the drums: "dom, dom, dom, dom."

4. Invite students to listen to the Spanish words in the song that have been displayed on the board or overhead projector, such as "aldea" (village), "iglesia" (church), "tambor" (drum), and "día" (day).

5. Learn to sing the song through the process of immersion, listening repeatedly to the recording (or to the teacher), singing the phrases that are more comfortable, and gradually adding phrases until the song is known in its entirety.

6. Reinforce the interval of a minor third (d-F) by singing measures 9–12 and 21–24. Compare the sound to a major third (d-F♯).

7. Add the pitched ostinati on xylophones and metallophones, as indicated. Practice singing the song first with one ostinato, and then add instrumental parts with each repetition.

8. Add the drums and maracas to the ensemble, playing them softly to allow the metallophones to ring clearly as if they were the church bells of "la iglesia en la plaza."

9. Extend the cultural adventure by encouraging students to investigate the country of Guatemala and to report on Guatemala's geography, the history of its Native and Spanish people, its economy, and its principal holiday celebrations.

Tamborcita

Classroom Instrumental Arrangement

Guatemala

Wait for intro.

All measures ostinati
(play same pattern throughout)

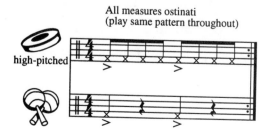

high-pitched

El Barreño
(The Earthen Bowl)

About the Song

Guatemala is among the most heavily agrarian societies in Latin America. More than half the people live as their ancestors did: residing in small towns and villages and farming the land. Like rural societies the world over, Guatemalans allow music into their lives while working in the fields and when gathering with families and neighbors. The songs that originate in the fields become the melodies of the marimbas that play for singing and dancing. Guatemalans play three types of marimbas: the marimba de tecomates (marimba with gourds), the marimba sencilla (with 33 to 40 keys or bars), and the marimba doble (the largest, which has 68 keys or bars and accommodates up to four musicians). Once the music begins to play, the singing and dancing may carry on well into the night. "El Barreño" is a traditional melody of Guatemala, sung by Lucía Quintana and played by a marimba ensemble coordinated by Ethel Batrés of Guatemala City [20]. From the charleo, or buzzing sound, of the marimbas to the tremolo of the sustained tones, this is a fine example of authentic Guatemalan music.

El Barreño

Guatemala

Wait for intro. — Listen for the drums!
Verse 1:

De los ca - ba - *lli - tos que me tra - jo_us - ted, Nin - gu - no me gus - ta, Só - lo_el que mon -

té. Há - ga - se pa'_a - cá, há - ga - se pa'_a - llá, Que mi ca - ba - lli - to lo_a - tro - pe - lla -
(2.) ma - ta"_Ay ba - rre - ño sí, Ay ba - rre - ño no, Ay ba - rre - ño due - ño de mi co - ra -

rá. Há - ga - se pa'_a - cá, há - ga - se pa'_a - llá, Que mi ca - ba - lli - to lo_a - tro - pe - lla -
zón. Ay ba - rre - ño sí, Ay ba - rre - ño no, Ay ba - rre - ño due - ño de mi co - ra -

Fine *Verse 2:*

rá.
zón.   Por a_hí vie - ne_un le - che - ri - to, con su cán - ta - ro de

D.S. al Fine

pla - ta.   Y la ni - ña le res - pon - de: "E - sa le - che_a mí me

* pronunciation: ll = "zh"

The Song Text

Verse 1:

De los caballitos que me trajo usted,
Day lohs kah-bah-zhee-tos kay may trah-hoo-stehd

Ninguno me gusta, solo el que monté.
Neen-goo-noh may goo-stah soh-lo-ehl kay mohn-tay

Hágase pa' aca, hágase pa' allá,
Ah-gah-say pah-kah, ah-gah-say pah-zhah,

Que mi caballito lo atropellará.
Kay mee kah-bah-zhee-toh loah-troh-peh-zhah-shh (Repeat last two lines)

Verse 2:

Por ahí viene un lecherito,
Pohr ah-ee byehn-nayn leh-cheh-ree-toh

Con su cántaro de plata.
Kohn soo kahn-tah-roh day plah-tah

Y la niña le responde:
Ee lah nee-nah leh rehs-pohn-day

Esa leche a mí me mata.
Eh-sah lay-chaya mee may mah-

Ay barreño sí, ay barreño no,
-Tay bah-ray-noh see, ay bah-ray-noh noh

Ay barreño dueño de mi corazón.
Ay bah-ray-noh dway-noh day mee koh-rah-zohn (Repeat last two lines)

Text in English

Verse 1:

Of all the little horses that you brought me,
I don't like any of them except the one that I rode.
Come over here, go over there,
(Or that) the little horse will run you down.

Verse 2:

A little milkman arrives with his silver can of milk,
And the young girl responds: "I love that milk!"
Oh, the bowl, yes. Oh, the bowl, no.
Oh, I adore my bowl.

Teaching Suggestions

1. Refer to Teaching Suggestions 1 and 2 from "Tamborcita" for setting the geographic and cultural context of "El Barreño." Draw attention to the images of village life in Guatemala that are found in the song, from the "little horses" (caballitos) to the "little milkman" (lecherito).

2. While listening to the song, follow the prominent feeling of triple meter. The opening section features a steady quarter-note pulse in the bass marimba, which students can conduct in a three-beat pattern. A break in the marimbas occurs while a new percussion pattern is laid out, followed by the entrance of marimbas again into the new rhythmic swing.

3. Listen several times: (a) to the marimbas, their tremolo on sustained notes, the close harmony of thirds, the charleo (buzzing sound), and the separate part of the bass marimba; (b) to the text (the sections that begin with "hágase" and "ay barreño" are perhaps the easiest to learn due to the repetition of the text).

4. Select several phrases that are in effect chordal outlines (do-mi-do-mi-so in measures 5–6 and 9–10) or examples of melodic sequence (measures 14–15, 16–17, and 18–19), and sing them with hand signs.

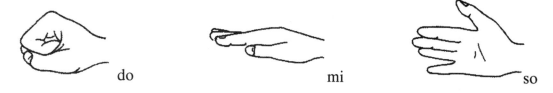

do   mi   so

5. Learn the song, beginning with "hágase" and "ay barreño" sections that function as refrains to the verse. It's important to allow singers to feel the rhythm and to come gradually into more accurate pitch-matching; the language will find its way into the singing through repeated listening and practice.

6. Play the instrumental accompaniment on xylophones (soprano, alto, and bass) and on drum and claves or woodblock. The accompaniment can be played as an introduction, interlude, and coda to the song, and the two sung verses (and refrains) can be sung several times to extend the song to a performance piece.

7. Explore, compare, and contrast "xylophone cultures" such as those found in Indonesia, Zimbabwe, and Guatemala. How are the xylophones constructed? What does their music sound like? How are these traditions similar? How are they distinctive?

El Barreño
Classroom Instrumental Arrangement

Wait for intro with drums.

Guatemala

0562B

Mexico

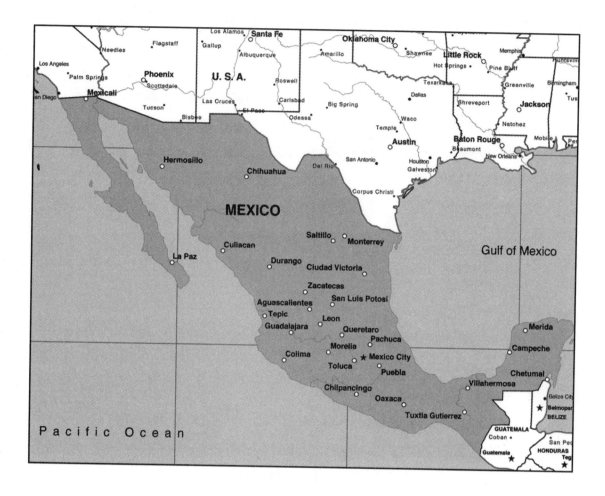

As Mexican cuisine has become standard meal-fare in many parts of the world, so has the music of this colorful nation become known well beyond its borders. In parts of North America, Latin America, and even Europe, the appeal of the Mexican-style burrito or taco is matched by the sound of mariachi, música ranchera, música jarocha, and the classical music of Silvestre Revueltas, Manuel Ponce, and Carlos Chávez. More than 100 million citizens of Mexico can't be wrong! Live singing and instrumental forms of music are important to celebrations for baptism, quince años (a debutante celebration for 15-year-olds), weddings, birthdays, and holidays. The musical life of Mexico is a panorama of popular, artistic, folk, and indigenous expressions that reflect the pluralism of the Mexican population as well as international influences that Mexicans have reshaped to create their own unique styles.

The Musical Surroundings: Getting to Know Mexico

Land and People. Mexico is erroneously viewed as part of Central America, when in fact it is the southern third of the North American landmass that includes Canada and the United States. It is three times the size of the state of Texas and has varying climates that include the dry desert of the north, the cooler central plateau (where Mexico City, its capital, is located) bounded by two mountain ranges, and the tropical jungle of the south. Mexico's history can be traced to the Olmecs from around 2000 B.C.; to the Mayan Empire, which fell in the twelfth century; and to the Aztecs, who were conquered by the Spanish in 1521. Mexico was one of the first countries to revolt against Spain in a drive led by priest Miguel Hidalgo, with independence coming in 1821. Mexico had considerable growing pains, with Texas seceding in 1836, further loss of its northwestern territory after a war with the U.S. from 1846–48, a French invasion in 1861, an Austrian archduke as emperor for six years, dictator Porfirio Díaz in power until his overthrow in 1910, and more political unrest in the 1920s and '30s. A democracy functioned for the remainder of the century, but the ruling Institutional Revolutionary Party was considerably weakened in the 1990s by several rebel movements protesting government policy regarding indigenous people. About 30 percent of the population are Indian, mostly descendents of the Maya and Aztecs; 60 percent are mestizo (mixed Spanish and Indian descent); and about 9 percent are of European heritage. More than one-quarter of the population live in the vicinity of Mexico City and within sight of the active Popocatépetl volcano.

Economy. The two most important industries of Mexico, mining and petroleum, employ less than two percent of the labor force. Tourism provides employment for many. Mexico exports oil, coffee, agricultural products, and engines. Major crops include corn, cotton, wheat, and coffee. Political shocks in the 1990s led to a deep financial crisis, although NAFTA (the North American Free Trade Agreement) with the United States and Canada has helped lower trade barriers and has led to an increased number of maquiladoras (border industries).

Education. School is free and compulsory for children between the ages of six and fourteen. Attendance is not enforced, however, and students must pay fees at some schools. The average adult literacy rate is 89 percent, although it is much lower among indigenous and rural populations.

Language. Spanish is the official language of Mexico. A common characteristic is the use of diminutives, such as when *chico* (small) becomes *chiquito* (tiny), and *abuelo* (grandfather) becomes *abuelito*. More than one hundred Indian languages are spoken, including Tzeltal (Mayan dialect), Nahuatl (Aztec), Otomi, and Mixtec.

Customs and Courtesies. Mexicans greet with a handshake or nod of the head, although friends commonly embrace. Common verbal greetings include "Buenos días" (Good morning), "¿Cómo está" (How are you?), and "Hola" (Hi). Mexican males often make piropos (flattering personal comments) in passing to women, although the women seldom respond. Mexicans have more than one given name and two surnames, for example, María Ana Martínez Salina, the first surname coming from the father and the second from the mother. Often in conversation, Mexicans touch their friends' clothing and use their hands and arms in gestures. Indians are more reserved, conversing with little physical contact and touching their mouths or cheeks when they speak. If someone sneezes, a person may say "Salud" (Good health). If one passes between conversing individuals, it is polite to say "Con permiso" (Excuse me). It is important to express thanks for any favor or commercial service ("Gracias").

Appearance. Most Mexicans dress in clothing commonly found in other parts of North America. In some areas, men wear wool ponchos (sarapes) over their shirts and pants when it is cold, and sometimes wide-brimmed straw hats. Rural men in the north may wear cowboy hats, boots, and jeans, and rural women often wear dresses or skirts covered by an apron. They may also use shawls (rebozos) to carry children or to cover their heads.

Families. The trend for Mexicans is to have smaller families, but it is still common to see families of three or more children. In traditional families, the father is the family leader and provides economic support while the mother is responsible for domestic and childcare duties. Rural men and women work together in the fields. Children generally live with their parents until they marry and sometimes after they are married.

Recreation. Soccer (fútbol) is the most popular sport in Mexico, and the national team has competed in the last five World Cups. Bullfighting draws the second highest number of spectators. Professional wrestling (la lucha) has a large following, as does a form of rodeo called charreada. Daylong fiestas and weeklong festivals nearly always feature a mariachi band or other musical group. Soap operas (telenovelas) are popular, along with other television viewing.

Food. In traditional Mexico, lunch is the main meal of the day; urban professionals often eat meals at restaurants or street-side stands. Staple foods include corn, beans, rice, and chilies, which are combined with spices, vegetables, and meat or fish. Common foods are cornmeal or flour tortillas, quesadillas (tortillas baked or fried with cheese), mole (spicy sauce), and tacos (folded tortillas with meat or other fillings). Picante (hot, spicy foods) are often eaten with bland foods such as bread, tortillas, or rice to relieve any burning sensation.

Holidays. National public holidays include New Year's Day; Constitution Day (February 5), which is also the beginning of Carnaval; the Birthday of Benito Juárez (March 21); Cinco de Mayo (May 5), which celebrates an 1867 victory over the French; Independence Day (September 16), which is marked by a presidential address and El Grito (the cry of freedom) on the evening of September 15; Revolution Day (November 20); and Christmas Day. Religious holidays include St. Anthony's Day (January 17), when children take animals to church to be blessed, and Semana Santa (Palm Sunday through Easter Sunday). During Día de los Muertos (Day of the Dead) on November 1–2, families gather to celebrate life and honor the dead by sweeping the graves of and building altars for those who have recently passed away. The Day of the Virgin Guadalupe (December 12) is so popular that most businesses close to honor it as a public holiday. Christmas celebrations begin with nightly parties (posadas) and end on the Day of the Kings (January 6).

Adelita
(Adelita)

About the Song

Along with the "standard" or characteristic exported Mexican sound of guitars, violins, and trumpets of the mariachi, there are many combinations of these and other instruments that play for rural dances, birthdays, and holiday occasions. The best known of the songs they play (at least to English-speaking foreigners) are "Jarabe Tapatío" (sometimes referred to as the "Mexican Hat Dance") and "La Cucaracha," but the repertoire of Mexican instrumental groups is far more expansive. Historical events, imagined people, and the romantic spirit weave in and out of many of the texts of the songs they play. One of the favorite songs of Mexicans is "Adelita," a tribute to a brave and beautiful girl. Although not a real person, Adelita symbolizes the ideal woman in the imagination of soldiers (a universal theme in songs of soldiers from many cultures). María de León Arcila, singer, is accompanied by Jorge A. Jara de León on guitar, Alejandra on salterio (a plucked dulcimer), and Héctor Larios on accordion, all from Santiago de Querétaro, Mexico ⊕ .

Adelita

Mexico

Verse 1:

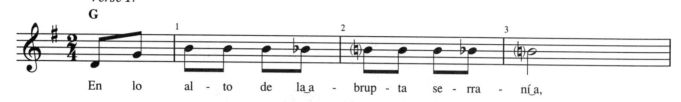

En lo al - to de la a - brup - ta se - rra - ní_a,

A - cam - pan - do se_en - con - tra - ba_un re - gi - mien - to.

Y_u - na mo - za que va - lien - te lo se - guí - a, Lo - ca -

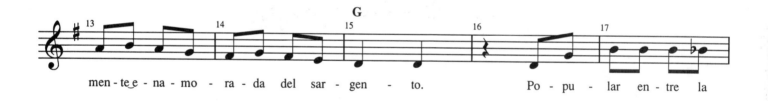

men - te_e - na - mo - ra - da del sar - gen - to. Po - pu - lar en - tre la

tro - pa e_ra A - de - li - ta. La mu - jer que_al sar - gen - to_i - do - la -

tra - ba, Por - que_a más de ser va - lien - te e_ra bo -

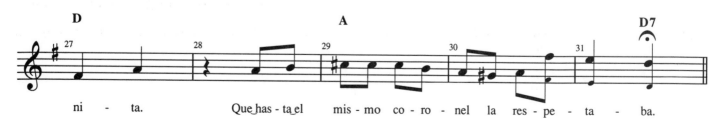

ni - ta. Que_has - ta_el mis - mo co - ro - nel la res - pe - ta - ba.

The Song Text

Verse 1:

En lo alto de la abrupta serranía,
Ehn loh ahl-toh day lah-bruhp-tah seh-rah-nee-ah

Acampando se encontraba un regimiento.
Ah-cahm-pahn-doh say-kohn-trah-bahn reh-hih-mee-ehn-toh

Y una moza que valiente lo seguía,
Yoo-nah moh-sah kay vah-lee-ehn-tay lo seh-gee-ah

Locamente enamorada del sargento.
Lok-ah-mehn-tayn-ah-moh-rah-dah del sahr-hen-toh

Popular entre la tropa era Adelita.
Poh-poo-lahr ehn-tray lah troh-peh rah-dehl-lee-tah

La mujer que al sargento idolatraba,
Lah moo-hehr kay a sahr-hehn-toy-doh-la-trah-bah

Porque a más de ser valiente era bonita.
Pohr-kaya-mahs day sehr vah-lee-ehn-tay-rah boh-nee-tah

Que hasta el mismo coronel la respetaba.
Kyahs-tahl mees-moh coh-roh-nehl lah rehs-peh-tah-bah

Interlude:

Y se oía, que decía, aquel que tanto la quería
Ee sayoh-ee-ah, kay deh-see-ah, ah-kayl kay tahn-toh lah keh-ree-ah

Verse 2:

Que si Adelita se fuera con otro,
Kay seeah-deh-lee-tah say fweh-rah kohn oh-troh

La seguiría por tierra y por mar.
Lah seh-gee-ree-ah pohr tee-ehr-rah ee pohr mahr

Si por mar, en un buque de guerra,
See pohr mahr ehn oon boo-kay day gehr-rah

Si por tierra en un tren militar.
See pohr tee-eh-rahn oon trehn mee-lee-tahr

Y si Adelita quisiera ser mi novia,
Ee see ah-deh-lee-tah kee-see-eh-rah sehr mee noh-vee-ah

Y si Adelita fuera mi mujer,
Ee see ah-deh-lee-tah foo-eh-rah mee moo-hehr

Le compraría un vestido de seda,
Leh cohm-prah-ree-ahn vehs-tee-doh day say-dah

Para llevarla a bailar al cuartel.
Pah-rah yeh-vahr-lah by-lahr ahl kwahr-tel

Text in English

Verse 1:

On the top of a rugged hill

A regiment of soldiers was camping,

And a brave girl followed them

Since she was in love with the sergeant.

Adelita was popular among the soldiers.

She was adored by the sergeant

Because she was as brave as she was beautiful.

The colonel respected her, too.

And those who knew her loved and respected her.

Verse 2:

If Adelita were to go away with another,

I would follow by land and by sea.

If by sea, in a battleship,

And if by land, in a military train.

If Adelita wanted to be my girlfriend,

And if Adelita were to become my wife,

I would buy her a silk dress,

And take her dancing at the military ball.

Teaching Suggestions

1. Note the location of Mexico on a map, and challenge students to consider the suggestion of Mexico as geographically belonging to North America while culturally more connected to Central America. Probe the history of Mexico, and look for events and influences that would have connected the country to Central America, the United States, the Caribbean, Europe, and other parts of the world.

2. Scan the text and display and pronounce Spanish words that appear, such as "regimiento" (soldiers), "porque" (because), "valiente" (brave), "bonita" (beautiful), "tierra" (land), "con otro" (with another), "mar" (sea), "quisiera" (I want/I wish), "mujer" (woman, wife), "bailar" (to dance). Use these and other Spanish words in conversation until students find them familiar and meaningful.

3. Listen to the recording of "Adelita," and invite students to join in keeping a lively two-beat in any number of ways. Suggest a pat-clap or a clap-snap gesture for the 1-2 of each measure, but consider also a waist bend to the right and left, a right- and then left-foot tap, or even walking to the beat in a circle (or randomly across the floor). Encourage free movement at the interlude.

4. Ask students to listen carefully for words they have learned (see #2). In another listening, show the Spanish-language verse with familiar words highlighted or underlined.

5. Sing such patterns as (a) "so-do-mi," (b) "do-mi-so," and (c) "so-do-mi-so," all combinations of pitches of the tonic chord, using hand signs (see page 65). Listen for their occurrence in the song: (a) pickup-mm. 1 and 16–17, (b) mm. 4–5 and 20–21, (c) mm. 38–39 and 62–63. For this activity, ignore the cue-sized notes, which are optional notes for singing, in case the vocal ranges are too high for some students.

6. This song is more difficult to sing than the other songs in this collection. Feel free to omit the complete singing of the song from your lesson and focus on the other activities. If you choose to learn to sing the song, sing repeatedly with the recording or to a lively accompaniment on guitar. The more difficult text may require isolation of individual lines or phrases that can be heard and then sung repeatedly until mastered.

7. An instrumental accompaniment can be added featuring guitar(s) with several classroom instruments: maracas, conga drum, guiro, and ratchet.

8. The music invites dancing. Students can form an inner and an outer circle, paired and facing each other.

Introduction: Partners face one another and bow and curtsy to each other.

(1) Measures 1–4: Outer circle turns right and steps eight counts to the right.
   Measures 5–8: Inner circle turns left and steps eight counts to their left (facing partner).

(2) Measures 9–12: Outer circle steps eight counts to their left, to their original place.
   Measures 13–16: Inner circle steps eight counts to their right (facing partner again), to their original place.

(3) Measures 17–20: Partners form arms in a "skater's position" (crossed in front), and step eight counts to the outer circle's right.

Measures 21–24: Partners step back eight counts to original place (in skater's position).

(4) Measures 25–28: Partners face one another, take hands, and switch places, followed by a curtsy or bow.

Measures 29–32: Partners switch places again and curtsy and bow.

For the **interlude**, partners stretch arms to the outside circle right (four counts), to the outside circle left (four counts), and then do a "dish-rag" movement in which partners face each other holding hands, then raise hands to walk under each other, and emerge back in original position (four counts).

The movement of steps 1–4 is repeated with each verse.

9. A simpler "dance" is to step individually to the pulse of the music, changing directions every 16 counts. At the interlude, individuals find a partner, lock arms in a skater's position, and move together for the second verse. Individual and partner sections are repeated with each following verse.

10. How many different perspectives are there of Mexico, its geography, culture, artistic expressions, and musical expressions? Meet the challenge of searching out the variety in this Latin American country, considering the variety within every Latin American country.

Adelita

Classroom Instrumental Arrangement

* Guitarist should see song with lyrics for chord changes.

De Colores
(Colors)

About the Song

Poets, musicians, and painters have been inspired by the beauty of a spring countryside, when in some climates the green of the grass and trees is fresher and more alive than ever and when the flowers blossom in colorful celebration. Mexico has its own song of spring, a traditional favorite for generations: "De Colores." It is a pleasing song, contagious for its gentle metric swing, its lyrical melody, and the ease with which harmonies flow in layered thirds atop the melody. The song traveled with Mexicans to the United States through migrant workers in the vineyards and orchards of California and other western states and became integral to Chicano identity in the 1960s. Listen to "De Colores" and enjoy the lively rhythm on the guitar and percussion instruments.

De Colores

Mexico
(Mexican Amercian)

Wait for intro.
Verse 1:

De_____ co - lo - res,_____ de co - lo - res se vis - ten los cam - pos en la pri - ma -

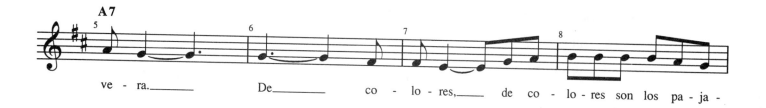

ve - ra._____ De_____ co - lo - res,_____ de co - lo - res son los pa - ja -

ri - tos que vie - nen de a - fue - ra._____ De_____ co - lo - res,_____ de co -

lo - res es el ar - co i - ris que ve - mos lu - cir._____ Y por

e - so los gran - des a - mo - res de mu - chos co - lo - res me gus - tan a mí.

The Song Text
Verse 1:

De colores,
Day koh-loh-rehs

De colores se visten los campos en la primavera.
Day koh-loh-rehs say vees-tehn lohs kahm-pohs ehn lah pree-mah-veh-ra

De colores,
Day koh-loh-rehs

De colores son los pajaritos que vienen de afuera.
Day koh-loh-rehs sohn los pah-jah-ree-tohs kay veehn-nehn day ah foo-ehr-ah

Verse 2:

De colores,
Day koh-loh-rehs

De colores es al arco iris que vemos lucir.
Day koh-loh-rehs ehs ahl ahr-koh ee-rees kay vay-mohs loo-seer

Y por eso los grandes amores de muchos colores
Ee pohr eh-soh lohs grahn-dehs ah-moh-rehs day moo-chos koh-loh-rehs

Me gustan a mi.
May goos-tahn ah mee

Text in English
Verse 1:

The colors,
The colors of countryside in the spring.
The colors,
The colors appear as the sun shines through the rain clouds.

Verse 2:

The colors,
The colors of the rainbow that appears when a storm cloud is touched by the sun...
And this great love of many colors
Is pleasing to me.

Teaching Suggestions

1. Refer to Suggestion #1 from "Adelita" in setting the song in its geographic location.

2. Show the Spanish-language text, and challenge students to select cognate words (words in Spanish that are similar to English): "colores" (colors), "campos" (country, countryside, [camp]), "iris" (iris, the blue flower), "arco" (arc) and "arco iris" (rainbow), "grande" (great).

3. While listening to the song, hear and feel the triple beat of the 6/8 meter by creating gestures for the pattern:

1	2	3	1	2	3
pat	clap	clap	pat	clap	clap
(lap)	(tap two fingers into hand)		(chest)	(tap two fingers into hand)	

Try this sitting down, and then convert it to a stepping-and-clapping pattern:

1	2	3	1	2	3
step	clap	clap	step	clap	clap
	(tap two fingers into hand)			(tap two fingers into hand)	

Convert the "1-2-3-1-2-3" counting to "1-2-3-4-5-6."

4. Sing the melody on a neutral syllable, such as "loo," and conduct the meter in two (down on 1 and up on 4 if you count six beats per measure). Clap the rhythm ♩ ♩ ♪ ♪ ♪, which appears in measures 1–2, 6–7, and 11–12. When this is comfortable to do sitting (or "in place"), try it while walking, stepping on beats 1 and 4.

5. Learn to sing the song, keeping the lyrical flow to the melody as smooth when singing the words as when singing on the neutral syllable.

6. Play the instrumental accompaniment on soprano, alto, and bass xylophones and alto glockenspiel. Add also the tambourine and guitar. As a performance piece, consider alternating between pitched percussion accompaniment (xylophones and glockenspiel) and guitar(s). An introduction and conclusion can be constructed from this accompaniment by playing the final four measures.

7. Trace the migration of Mexico—and its music and cultural expressions—to other parts of the Americas. In particular, consider the influences of Mexican migration to North America and the Chicano or Mexican-American presence or "movement."

De Colores
Classroom Instrumental Arrangement

Mexico
(Mexican American)

* Guitarist should see above for chord changes.

0562B

Puerto Rico

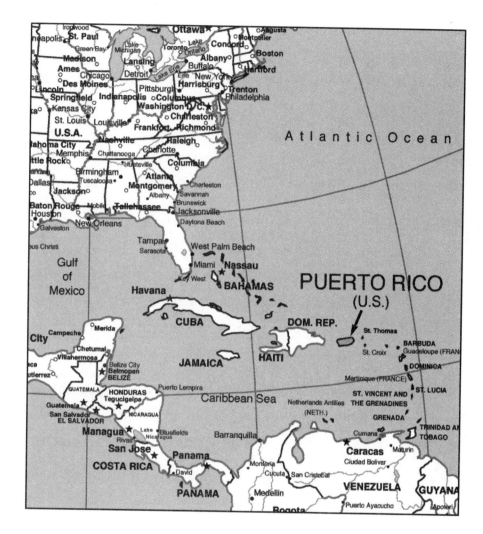

Along with the popular phenomenon of Ricky Martin and the legendary sound of Tito Puente (both American citizens of Puerto Rican ancestry), there is a continued strong musical presence among all Puerto Ricans. Music on the island and in U.S. communities of Puerto Ricans has been shaped by the multiple Taíno, Spanish, and African expressions that stand alone and blend together. From the Taíno come percussion instruments such as maracas and the güiro. From the Spanish are the string and wind instruments, their harmonies, and forms like the danza; and from the Africans are syncopations, cross-rhythms, and conga drums and timbales (open-ended drums played with untapered sticks). Music rules in the lives of Puerto Ricans, from the cello of Pablo Casals (born in Spain to a Puerto Rican mother) to bomba and plena music, children's songs, and the salsa music of Willie Colón, Héctor Lavoe, and the Fania All Stars.

The Musical Surroundings: Getting to Know Puerto Rico

Land and People. The island of Puerto Rico sits squarely in the middle of the Caribbean Sea and enjoys a mildly tropical climate. Columbus arrived in 1493 to claim the island for Spain, although it was inhabited by the indigenous Taíno people. African slaves were brought there beginning in 1513, and only in 1873 was slavery abolished. In 1897, Spain granted self-rule to Puerto Rico, but it was invaded in 1898 by the United States, who conquered the remaining members of the Spanish governing force. In 1917, Puerto Rico officially became a U.S. territory, and its people were granted citizenship. In 1952, Puerto Rico became a commonwealth of the U.S. with its own constitution. Today's Puerto Ricans, 95 percent of whom are of an undetermined mixed heritage of Spanish, African, and Taíno, are divided by the issue of whether or not to request U.S. statehood. About 3.8 million live on the island, and more than two million live in the U.S. (mostly in or surrounding New York City).

Economy. The once-poor agrarian island transformed into a dynamic economy, largely due to industrialization and duty-free trade with the United States. Government, services, tourism, and manufacturing provide most employment on the island. Puerto Rico exports sugar, coffee, petroleum products, textiles, and chemicals. The U.S. dollar is the official currency of Puerto Rico.

Education. Primary and secondary schooling is available for children ages five through eighteen, similar to the United States, and education is highly valued. The dropout rate is very low, and most students attain high school diplomas. The adult literacy rate is 89 percent and is higher among youths than adults.

Language. Spanish and English are official languages of Puerto Rico; Spanish is the language of school and daily life, while English is required as a second language and is used in business. Many Puerto Ricans mix English words with Spanish, creating a style of speech called Spanglish.

Customs and Courtesies. People shake hands when greeting or in a more familiar way grasp shoulders and kiss each other on the cheek. People stand very close when talking, and moving away may be considered an insult. Both Spanish and English greetings are heard: "Good morning" or "Buenos días," and "Hi" and "Hola." Young friends often begin a conversation with "¿Qué tal?" (How are you?). Friends address each other by given name or nickname, but adults in formal situations will use "señor" (Mr.), "señora" (Mrs. or Ms.), "señorita" (Miss), "doctor/a" (Dr.), and so on. Most Puerto Ricans have two surnames in addition to one or two given names, but the second-to-last name is the most important; a person called Luis Morla Rios would be called Señor Morla. Women do not exchange names when they marry. One calls to another by waving all fingers with the palm down. Wiggling the nose can mean "What's going on?" A person can get another's attention by saying "Pssst," and this is common and not rude. (However, if a man does it to a woman, she will likely ignore him.) Men often smile and stare at women, but it is considered improper for a woman to smile indiscriminately at strangers.

Appearance. Puerto Ricans dress with pride in public. Young people favor North American sporty fashions. Sloppy, overly casual, or revealing dress is considered inappropriate. For most parties and social gatherings, formal clothing, with suits for men and dresses for women, is expected.

Families. The Puerto Rican family is close-knit and supportive. Extended families may live in the same neighborhood, but not in the same home, and there are frequent visits among relatives. Grandparents often provide childcare when both parents work. Extended family units have an average of three families. If families migrate, one parent may move first and establish a home before the rest of the family joins him or her.

Food. Rice and beans is the most commonly eaten main meal of Puerto Ricans. Other popular dishes include arroz con pollo (rice with chicken), bacalao con viandas (boiled cod with casave bread, which is made from the yucca root, and potatoes), and arroz con gandules y pernil (rice with roasted pig). Plantains, seafood, and fruit (pineapples, mangoes, papayas, grapefruit, and oranges) are common in the diet. People enjoy arroz con leche (rice pudding) and frituras (snack foods fried in oil).

Recreation. The favorite sport of Puerto Ricans is baseball, but people also enjoy basketball and volleyball. The arts enjoy a wide following, including literature and music, as well as scholarship. Families foster music and art in the home, and nearly everyone plays a musical instrument. Parties are replete with family members playing together or for one another. At celebrations, salsa, plena, bomba, and danza puertorriqueña are the most popular forms of merry-making.

Holidays. Puerto Ricans celebrate New Year's Day as part of the Christmas season, ending with the Day of the Three Kings (January 6). Puerto Ricans celebrate both national and U.S. holidays, including the Birth of Eugenio María de Hostos (January 11), the Abolition of Slavery (March 22), Easter, José de Diego's Birthday (third Monday in April), Luis Muñoz Rivera Day (July 17), Constitution Day (July 25), José Celso Barbosa's Birthday (July 28), All Souls Day (November 2), Discovery of Puerto Rico Day (November 19), Thanksgiving, and Christmas. During the Christmas season is the Parrandas, when groups of friends sing Christmas songs door-to-door for food and drinks. Every town honors its patron saint annually with several days of activities that include going to amusement parks, gambling, singing, dancing, religious ceremonies, and the selection of a beauty queen. Carnaval celebrations held before Lent feature monsters (vejigantes) who wear bells and elaborate papier-mâché masks with multiple horns and jokingly threaten to hit people on the head with a dried pig's bladder.

Arroz con Leche

About the Song

Food and music figure importantly in the hierarchy of components of cultural identity; the holidays that Puerto Ricans celebrate are ideal venues for sampling them both! For Puerto Rican children, "Arroz con Leche" is a playful song that combines the pleasures of Puerto Rican food with music. This song opens with praise for rice pudding but quickly sets up a game that children know well.

Arroz con Leche

Puerto Rico

1. A - rroz con le - che se quie - re ca - sar con
(2.) soy la viu - di - ta, la hi - ja del rey, Me

u - na viu - di - ta de la ca - pi - tal, que
quie - ro ca - sar y no en - cuen - tro con quien;

se - pa co - ser, que se - pa bor - dar; que
Con - ti - go sí, con - ti - go no, con -

pon - ga la me - sa en su_____ lu - gar. 2. Yo
ti - go mi vi - da, me ca - sa - ré yo.

The Song Text

Verse 1:

Arroz con leche se quiere casar
Ah-rohz kon lay-chay say kee-eh-ray cah-sar

Con una viudita de la capital
Kohn oo-nah vee-oo-dee-tah day lah kahp-ee-tahl

Que sepa coser, que sepa bordar;
Kay say-pah koh-sehr, kay say-pah bohr-dahr

Que ponga la mesa en su lugar.
Kay pohn-gah lah may-sah ehn soo loo-gahr

Verse 2:

Yo soy la viudita, la hija del rey.
Yoh soy lah vee-oo-dee-tah, lah ee-hah dehl ray

Me quiero casar y no encuentro con quien.
May kee-eh-roh kah-sahr ee no ehn-kwehn-troh kon kee-ehn

Contigo sí, contigo no,
Kohn-tee-goh see, kohn-tee-goh no

Contigo mi vida, me casaré yo.
Kohn-tee-goh mee vee-dah, may kah-sah-ray yo

Text in English

Verse 1:

Rice with milk (rice pudding) is good to eat
With a widow from the capital (city of San Juan)
Who knows how to cook and sew;
Who sets a fine table of foods.

Verse 2:

I am a widow, the daughter of a king.
I wish to choose a companion. With you, yes, with you, no,
With you I will enjoy life.

Teaching Suggestions

1. Find Puerto Rico on a world map, and trace a direct route Columbus might have taken to get there from Spain. Note the migration of Spaniards to Puerto Rico and neighboring islands. Imagine the most likely route Europeans took to bring West Africans to the island. Observe the distance from Puerto Rico to New York City, and, finally, consider the historical and contemporary relationships of Puerto Rico with other Caribbean and Latin American countries.

2. Discuss singing games that children know in terms of (a) their origin, (b) the meaning of their words, (c) how they are played, and (d) their melodies. Mention "Ring Around the Rosy" (English-speaking countries), "Leron, Leron" (the Philippines), "La Víbora de la Mar" (Mexico), "Cum Num Cum Niu" (Vietnam), "La Shevet" (Israel), "Miss Mary Mack" (U.S. African-American), "The Noble Duke of York" (English-speaking countries), "Sansa Kroma" (Ghana), "Kumbraza" (Eritrea), and "Zui Zui Zukkorobashi" (Japan), and others the children know, and compare them.

3. Listen to the recording of the song, and follow the contour of the melody by "drawing" in the air the rise and fall of pitches. In successive listenings, direct students to find the "so-do" in the melody and to use hand signs when they hear the pattern.

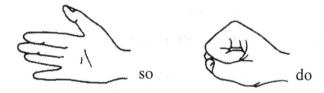

so   do

4. Have students learn to sing the song by singing with the recording and without it, and with the hand signs and "drawings" of the melodic contour and without them. These techniques help cue the attention of singers to more accurately match pitch.

5. Add the instrumental accompaniment, beginning with the pitched percussion, and then layer in the claves, cowbell, and two (conga) drums. Experiment with singing the melody with only the pitched percussion, then with only the unpitched percussion, and finally altogether.

6. The singing game is played by forming a circle and selecting someone to stand in the center. As the circle moves around, the center person mimes the words of a song. On "Contigo sí," the center person closes his or her eyes and with a pointed finger twirls around until the end of the second verse, when he/she selects a new center person ("Contigo mi vida, me casaré yo.").

7. Make the leap from a children's song to the music of which Puerto Ricans are rightly proud—salsa— by sampling Willie Colón, Tito Puente, and Eddie Palmieri, all of whom helped develop the genre in the Puerto Rican barrios (neighborhoods) of New York City.

Arroz con Leche

Classroom Instrumental Arrangement

Puerto Rico

0562B

Venezuela

Venezuelan music is lively, so lively that even at a sit-down formal concert of traditional music, audience members often can be heard rapidly tapping their feet to the rhythms of a guitar, violin, full-sized floor-model harp, cuatro (four-string guitar-like instrument), and maracas—played alone or in some combination. Given its location on the north coast of South America, Venezuela's music has more than a tinge of Caribbean sound in its salsa, merengue, and cumbia styles. But it is more than that: it is gaitas and aguinaldos (traditional Christmas music), joropos (traditional music of los llaneros, or cowboys, of the central plains), tonadas, and evolutions of the Spanish fandango—all of which feature lively rhythmic nuances. Venezuela's music includes the expressions of the Spanish, the indigenous, the mestizo (mixed) populations, and the black Africans and mulattos (mixed European and black peoples of the coastal regions). "Pure" and unblended sounds are rare, except in the European classical music scene in Caracas, while the mixing of African and Spanish expressions are far more common.

The Musical Surroundings: Getting to Know Venezuela

Land and People. There are four geographic zones of Venezuela: the Andes Mountains of the west, the northern coast, the large central plain east of the Orinoco River, and the high plateaus and jungle of the south. Angel Falls, the highest waterfall in the world, is located in the southeast, and a reserve for the Yanomami Indians is found in the far south. Columbus arrived in 1498, entering a region already inhabited by the Arawaks, Caracas, and other indigenous groups. The Spanish named the region Venezuela (little Venice) because the coastal homes built on stilts reminded them of Venice, Italy. Spain governed until Venezuelans won their independence in 1821, much to the credit of liberator Simón Bolívar. Venezuela experienced dictatorships, instability, and military coups for nearly a century, but a freely elected president came to power in 1958. Several decades of prosperity due to Venezuela's oil wealth were followed by plummeting oil prices, causing increased inflation and unemployment. A succession of presidents have been challenged to stabilize the economy. While Venezuela is blessed with great natural beauty, it remains the most urbanized country in South America; more than 90 percent of the people live in urban areas. More than two-thirds of the population are mestizo (mixed Spanish and Indian heritage), 21 percent are either of Italian or Spanish descent or mulatto. Another ten percent are black, and two percent are indigenous.

Economy. Venezuela's economic rise and fall reflects the world's oil prices, since its oil reserves are among the largest in the world. It is a member of OPEC (Organization of Petroleum Exporting Countries), and 80 percent of all export earnings and more than half of all government revenues are from petroleum. Agriculture employs only ten percent of the population and produces grain, sugar, and fruit. The gap between the rich and the poor is widening as Venezuela's middle class continues to shrink; nearly 80 percent of its people live in poverty.

Education. School is compulsory (though not enforced) from ages seven to fourteen. All education, including university, is free in public institutions. About three-fourths of all students complete nine years of primary school, and most go on to two years of secondary school. The adult literacy rate is 92 percent.

Language. Spanish is spoken throughout the country, except among Indians living in remote areas (such as the Yanomami). There are colloquialisms in the Spanish, however, not found elsewhere. For example, *chévere* means "cool" or "very well," and *estar pelado* (to be bald) can also mean "to be broke." English is a required study in secondary schools.

Customs and Courtesies. Men greet close friends with an abrazo (a full embrace while patting each other on the back), and women greet and part with an abrazo and a kiss on the cheek. Conversations occur with the speakers in close proximity, and backing away is improper; in the Andes region, however, some distance is preferred. Acquaintances and professionals are addressed by title (Doctor, Señor, Señora) usually followed by the surname. Venezuelans use their hands during conversation:

they will, for example, ask the price of an item or request payment by rubbing the thumb and index finger together while rotating the palm up. Pointing with the index finger is considered rude, as is slouching or propping up the feet upon any object.

Appearance. In all levels of society, it is important to look one's best and be properly groomed. Venezuelans are fashion-conscious: urban people wear the latest European styles. Native peoples may wear European or traditional dress or a combination of both.

Families. Family ties are strong, and most families are close-knit. However, about half of all births in Venezuela are out of wedlock or in common-law marriages. The father dominates in the home, but the responsibility for raising the children and managing the household traditionally rests with the mother. Women comprise one-fifth of the labor force. If members of a family are affluent, they typically share their wealth with less fortunate members.

Recreation. The most popular sports in Venezuela are baseball and basketball, with horse racing and bullfighting also attracting many fans. Many women enjoy walking, cycling, and playing softball. Venezuelans like to go dancing, to the movies, to the beach, and to the mountains. Playing dominoes and visiting friends and relatives are favorite leisure activities.

Food. Families traditionally eat together for midday and evening meals, although this practice has been abandoned in larger cities. Common foods in Venezuela include pasta, rice, beans, plantains, white cheese, chicken, potatoes, and fish. Corn is the basis of many dishes, and fried foods are popular. One favorite is the arepa, a deep-friend pancake sometimes filled with cheese or meat; hayacas are arepas stuffed with meat, potatoes, olives, raisins, and spices. Popular fruits include mangoes, lechosa (papaya), bananas, and watermelon.

Holidays. Many families vacation at the beach or in the mountains during Semana Santa, the week preceding Easter. Carnaval is celebrated with vigor, particularly in eastern Venezuela, where there are water fights, parades, and dancing in the streets. Towns and cities hold annual ferias (festivals) honoring the local patron saint. Other holidays include New Year's Day, Declaration of Independence Day (April 19), Battle of Carabobo (June 24), Independence Day (July 5), Simón Bolívar's birthday (July 24), and Christmas. Flowers are important in Venezuelan celebrations, and on holidays, the statues of Simón Bolívar, the father of Venezuela, are decorated with colorful wreaths.

Llegó Diciembre
(December Has Arrived)

About the Song

December is one of the few months of the year that boasts its own song forms. For cultures in which Christianity is influential, this may be due to the timing of the Christmas season, when gaitas and aguindaldos are frequently heard unaccompanied or with instruments. In this case, "gaita" refers to a Christmas song with instruments. In Venezuela, gaitas can be "sweet and low" or quite spirited, as is the case in "Llegó Diciembre," where a description of the season includes not only sights and sounds, but also the aromas of this magical time of year. The Octavo En-Re-Do ensemble of Caracas, Venezuela, perform "Llegó Diciembre" in a multipart vocal arrangement that alternates with a solo voice. Featured instruments in the ensemble are violin, cuatro, mandolin, guitar, stringed bass, drum, and maracas.

Venezuela

Lle-gó di-ciem-bre, con su gai-ta y su tam-bo-ra. Pa-ra los san-

tos, has-ta que a-lum-bre la au-ro-ra. Lle-gó di - la au-ro-ra. 1. Des-de el

tre-ce en la ma-ña-na; Ya es-tá re-ven-tan-do el dí-

a, Se en-cien-den los pa-la-fi-tos con gai-tas pa-ra Lu-cí-a.

0562B

The Song Text

Refrain:

Llegó diciembre
Yay-goh dee-see-ehm-bray

Con su gaita y su tambora
Kohn soo gahee-tayee soo tahm-boh-rah

Para los santos, hasta que alumbre la aurora.
*Pah-rah los sahn-tos ahs-tah kyah-loom-bray
  lah-roh-rah*

Llegó diciembre.
Yay-goh dee see-ehm-bray

Verse 1:

Desde el trece en la mañana,
Dehs-dayl tray-say ehn lah mah-nyah-nah

Ya está reventando el día.
Yahs-tah reh-vehn-tahndo ehl dee-ah

Se encienden los parafitos con gaitas para Lucía.
*Sayn-seehn-dehn lohs pah-rah-fee-tohs kohn
  gah-ee-tahs pah-rah Loo-see-yah*

Verse 2: *(Verses 2–4 can be heard on Track 24,
  but not on Track 12)*

Cántame la gaita primo,
Kahn-tah-may lah gah-ee-tah pree-moh

Repícame la tambora
Rep-ee-kah-may lah tahm-boh-rah

Que estoy cantando a Benito
Kay-stoy cahn-tahn-doah Bay-nee-toh

Con mi voz de fina aurora.
Kohn mee vos day fee-noh-roh-rah

Verse 3:

Con su manta y su anillo
Kohn soo mahn-tah ee soo ah-nee-yoh

Voz recia de cantadora
Vos reh-see-ah day cahn-tah doh-rah

Cantando desde noviembre
Kahn-tahn-doh dehs-day noh-vee-ehm-bray

A la Chinita Señora.
Ah lah Chee-nee-tah Seh-nyoh-rah

Verse 4:

Las flores y los aromas
Lahs floh-rays ee lohs ah-roh-mahs

Que brotan desde tu frente
Kay broh-tahn dehs-day too frehn-tay

Son jazmines y alelíes
Sohn yahs-mee-nehs ee ah-lay-lee-ehs

De los Santos Inocentes.
Day lohs sahn-toh Ee-noh-sehn-tays

Text in English

Refrain:

December has arrived
With its gaita and its drum
For the saints until the dawn shines.
December has arrived.

Verse 1:

Morning appears.
The day is bursting with energy.
The lights are lit
And there are songs for Lucía.

Verse 2:

Sing for me the gaita, brother,
Play the drum
That I am singing to Benito
With my voice of fine gold.

Verse 3:

With your blanket and your ring
Strong voice and sugar-coated song
Singing after November
To Mrs. Chinita.

Verse 4:

The flowers and the aromas
That spring from your forehead
Are jasmine and lilies
Of the holy innocents.

Llegó Diciembre

Classroom Instrumental Arrangement

Venezuela

All measures ostinati
(play same pattern throughout)

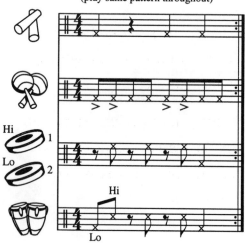

0562B

Teaching Suggestions

1. On a map of South America, find Venezuela and its neighbors, Colombia, Brazil, and Guyana. Note the Caribbean coast to the north and important bodies of water, Lake Maracaibo and the Orinoco River. Given its location and its populations of people of Spanish, Italian, mestizo, black African ancestry, and indigenous peoples, speculate as to the sounds that might comprise Venezuelan music.

2. Discuss Christmas celebrations in an assortment of families and cultures and the extent to which music and feasting play a part. In Venezuela, hayacas (deep-fried pancakes stuffed with meat, potatoes, olives, raisins, and spices) and Christmas music (gaitas and agüinaldos) are featured in the celebration.

3. In preparation for learning the song, and for extending a Spanish vocabulary, learn pronunciations and meanings for the following words: *diciembre* (December), *noviembre* (November), *tambora* (drum), *santos* (saints or holy), *aurora* (dawn), *mañana* (tomorrow, morning), *día* (day), *cantando* (singing), *flores* (flowers), *aromas* (aromas, scents), *manta* (blanket), *voz* (voice). Display these words prominently on the board or on an overhead projector and blend them into English conversation.

4. Look carefully at the verses, and note that the first verse refers to a specific genre called "gaita de Santa Lucía," which is a variation on a song in tribute to Santa Lucía, the patron saint of one parish in Maracaibo (on Lake Maracaibo) and whose feast day is December 13 (the "trece" in that verse). "Parafitos" are houses built on stilts out over the lake. Verse 2 refers to another genre of gaita called "gaita de tambor," which uses an ensemble of three to six conga-like drums in a very Afro-musical tribute to San Benito, the black saint from Italy, for whom several feast days are celebrated at Christmastide. "Repícame" is more than "ringing" a drum; it is idiomatic speech for "play a drum fill (improvisation) for me."

5. Listen to CD Track 24, keeping a steady pulse by patting the lap or the floor, and listen for the words as they appear in the song. Identify the instrument sounds, including violin, several stringed instruments (cuatro, mandolin, guitar), stringed bass, drum, and maracas. Determine the form of the song: Refrain, Verse 1, Verse 2, Interlude, Refrain, Verse 1, Verse 2, Refrain (twice).

6. Learn to sing the song, beginning with the recurring refrain. To avoid overloading the students, learn a new verse in each session, just keeping a steady pulse for the verses not yet directly learned (although some students will "pick up" these verses through the process of continued immersion).

7. Guitars and percussion make an acceptable accompaniment. Learn the rhythmic percussion ostinati one by one, chanting or counting and then playing the claves, maracas, higher-pitched drum, lower-pitched drum, and a third drum (preferably a conga) that plays both low and high pitches. An eighth-note guitar strum provides a steady chordal harmony.

8. Soprano, alto, and bass xylophones can provide harmony along with the guitars or in lieu of them. Note that there are just two four-beat patterns, so once they are learned, it will take only cueing and counting to determine which pattern goes where.

9. Investigate the nature of Christmas or December celebrations in Latin America. Are there special songs, foods, festivities elsewhere that are designated for the holiday? As for Venezuela, are there other music genres meant only for particular holidays?

Mucha alegría con estas canciones de América Latina
(Much Happiness With These Songs of Latin America)

Some say that a song is a window to the world of the singer and of a singing culture. These collected songs offer glimpses into worlds of people who prize music as an important expression of their identity, values, traditions, livelihoods, and even humor. From the opening of these windows to Latin American expressions may come grand openings of the portals, the double doors, and the gateways to this amazingly complex and colorful region of the world. We hope that those who listen to and learn these melodies, rhythms, and linguistic and cultural expressions will hold them in their hearts and will continue to pursue the musical avenues that lead to a fuller understanding of the people of Latin America.

Patricia Shehan Campbell